50 German Cake Flavor Recipes for Home

By: Kelly Johnson

Table of Contents

- Black Forest Cake (Schwarzwälder Kirschtorte)
- Bienenstich (Bee Sting Cake)
- Käsekuchen (German Cheesecake)
- Streuselkuchen (Crumb Cake)
- Apfelstrudel (Apple Strudel)
- Zitronenkuchen (Lemon Cake)
- Gugelhupf (Bundt Cake)
- Rhabarberkuchen (Rhubarb Cake)
- Nusstorte (Nut Cake)
- Linzer Torte
- Marzipan Torte
- Joghurtkuchen (Yogurt Cake)
- Karpatka (Carpathian Cake)
- Zwetschgenkuchen (Plum Cake)
- Donauwelle (Danube Wave Cake)
- Kaffekuchen (Coffee Cake)
- Heidelbeerkuchen (Blueberry Cake)
- Apfelkuchen (Apple Cake)
- Sachertorte
- Krapfen (German Doughnuts)
- Birnenkuchen (Pear Cake)
- Bienenstich Cupcakes
- Himbeerkuchen (Raspberry Cake)
- Hefezopf (Sweet Yeast Bread)
- Erdbeerkuchen (Strawberry Cake)
- Kokosnusstorte (Coconut Cake)
- Tropfen Kuchen (Droplet Cake)
- Kirschkuchen (Cherry Cake)
- Puddingkuchen (Pudding Cake)
- Schmandkuchen (Sour Cream Cake)
- Rote Grütze Cake
- Butterkuchen (Butter Cake)
- Bananenkuchen (Banana Cake)
- Zupfkuchen (Twist Cake)
- Pflaumenkuchen (Plum Cake)
- Marillenknödel (Apricot Dumplings)

- Marmorkuchen (Marble Cake)
- Eierlikörtorte (Egg Liqueur Cake)
- Quarktorte (Quark Cake)
- Pfeffernüsse (Pepper Nuts)
- Zitronenstreuselkuchen (Lemon Crumb Cake)
- Kirschenmichel (Cherry Michel)
- Joghurtkuchen mit Beeren (Yogurt Cake with Berries)
- Zebrakuchen (Zebra Cake)
- Kirschtorte (Cherry Torte)
- Wiener Apfelstrudel (Viennese Apple Strudel)
- Birnen-Schokoladenkuchen (Pear Chocolate Cake)
- Apfel-Mandelkuchen (Apple Almond Cake)
- Käsekuchen mit Streuseln (Cheesecake with Crumbs)
- Hasselback-Kuchen (Hasselback Cake)

Black Forest Cake (Schwarzwälder Kirschtorte)

Ingredients:

For the Cake:

- 2 cups (250g) all-purpose flour
- 1 1/2 teaspoons baking powder
- 1/2 teaspoon baking soda
- 1/2 cup (50g) unsweetened cocoa powder
- 1/2 cup (115g) unsalted butter, softened
- 1 cup (200g) granulated sugar
- 2 large eggs
- 1 cup (240ml) buttermilk
- 1 teaspoon vanilla extract

For the Cherry Filling:

- 1 jar (24 oz or 680g) Morello cherries, drained (reserve the juice)
- 1/4 cup (50g) granulated sugar
- 1 tablespoon cornstarch
- 1 tablespoon Kirsch (cherry schnapps), optional

For the Whipped Cream:

- 2 cups (480ml) heavy cream
- 1/4 cup (30g) powdered sugar
- 1 teaspoon vanilla extract

For Assembly:

- Chocolate shavings or grated chocolate, for decoration
- Fresh cherries with stems, for decoration

Instructions:

1. **Prepare the Cake:**
    1. Preheat your oven to 350°F (175°C). Grease and flour two 8-inch round cake pans.
    2. In a medium bowl, whisk together flour, baking powder, baking soda, and cocoa powder.
    3. In a large bowl, beat the softened butter and sugar until light and fluffy. Add eggs one at a time, beating well after each addition. Stir in the vanilla extract.
    4. Gradually add the dry ingredients to the butter mixture, alternating with the buttermilk, beginning and ending with the dry ingredients. Mix until just combined.
    5. Divide the batter evenly between the prepared pans and smooth the tops.

6. Bake for 25-30 minutes, or until a toothpick inserted into the center comes out clean. Let the cakes cool in the pans for 10 minutes, then turn out onto a wire rack to cool completely.

2. **Prepare the Cherry Filling:**
   1. In a medium saucepan, combine the drained cherries, sugar, and cornstarch. Cook over medium heat, stirring constantly, until the mixture thickens. Remove from heat and stir in Kirsch, if using. Let it cool.
3. **Prepare the Whipped Cream:**
   1. In a large bowl, beat the heavy cream, powdered sugar, and vanilla extract until stiff peaks form.
4. **Assemble the Cake:**
   1. Once the cakes are completely cooled, slice each cake in half horizontally to create four layers.
   2. Place one layer of cake on a serving plate. Spread a layer of cherry filling over it, then top with a layer of whipped cream.
   3. Repeat the layers, ending with a final layer of whipped cream on top.
   4. Decorate with chocolate shavings and fresh cherries.
5. **Chill and Serve:**
   1. Refrigerate the cake for at least 2 hours before serving to allow the flavors to meld.

Enjoy this deliciously layered and indulgent cake that brings a touch of German tradition to your table!

Bienenstich (Bee Sting Cake)

Ingredients:

For the Dough:

- 2 1/4 teaspoons (7g) active dry yeast
- 1/2 cup (120ml) warm milk
- 1/4 cup (50g) granulated sugar
- 1/4 cup (60g) unsalted butter, melted
- 1 large egg
- 2 1/2 cups (315g) all-purpose flour
- 1/4 teaspoon salt

For the Almond Topping:

- 1/4 cup (60g) unsalted butter
- 1/2 cup (100g) granulated sugar
- 2 tablespoons honey
- 1/4 cup (60ml) heavy cream
- 1 cup (100g) sliced almonds

For the Cream Filling:

- 1 cup (240ml) whole milk
- 1/2 cup (100g) granulated sugar
- 1/4 cup (30g) cornstarch
- 1/4 teaspoon salt
- 3 large egg yolks
- 2 tablespoons unsalted butter
- 1 teaspoon vanilla extract

Instructions:

1. **Prepare the Dough:**
    1. In a small bowl, dissolve the yeast in warm milk and let it sit for about 5 minutes, or until frothy.
    2. In a large bowl, mix together the sugar, melted butter, and egg. Add the yeast mixture and stir to combine.
    3. Gradually add the flour and salt, mixing until a soft dough forms.
    4. Knead the dough on a floured surface for about 5 minutes, or until smooth. Place the dough in a greased bowl, cover with a clean towel, and let it rise in a warm place for about 1 hour, or until doubled in size.
2. **Prepare the Almond Topping:**

1. In a medium saucepan, melt the butter over medium heat. Stir in the sugar, honey, and heavy cream. Bring to a simmer and cook for 2-3 minutes, until the mixture thickens slightly.
2. Remove from heat and stir in the sliced almonds. Set aside.

3. **Prepare the Cream Filling:**
   1. In a medium saucepan, whisk together the milk, sugar, cornstarch, and salt. Cook over medium heat, stirring constantly, until the mixture thickens and begins to boil.
   2. In a small bowl, lightly beat the egg yolks. Gradually add a small amount of the hot milk mixture to the yolks, stirring constantly. Pour the yolk mixture back into the saucepan and cook for an additional 2 minutes, stirring constantly.
   3. Remove from heat and stir in the butter and vanilla extract. Transfer the cream to a bowl, cover with plastic wrap (placing the wrap directly on the surface of the cream to prevent a skin from forming), and let it cool completely.
4. **Assemble the Cake:**
   1. Preheat your oven to 350°F (175°C). Grease and line a 9-inch round cake pan.
   2. Punch down the risen dough and transfer it to the prepared cake pan. Spread the dough evenly in the pan.
   3. Spoon the almond topping mixture evenly over the dough.
   4. Bake for 25-30 minutes, or until the cake is golden brown and a toothpick inserted into the center comes out clean.
   5. Let the cake cool completely in the pan on a wire rack.
5. **Fill the Cake:**
   1. Once the cake is completely cool, slice it in half horizontally.
   2. Spread the cooled cream filling evenly over the bottom layer of the cake. Place the top layer with the almond topping back on top.
6. **Serve:**
   1. Slice and serve the cake. It's best enjoyed fresh, but it can be stored in an airtight container at room temperature for up to 2 days.

Enjoy this sweet and crunchy treat that's a perfect blend of textures and flavors!

Käsekuchen (German Cheesecake)

Ingredients:

For the Crust:

- 1 1/2 cups (150g) graham cracker crumbs or digestive biscuits, crushed
- 1/4 cup (50g) granulated sugar
- 1/2 cup (115g) unsalted butter, melted

For the Filling:

- 2 cups (500g) quark (or use farmer's cheese or ricotta as a substitute)
- 1 cup (200g) granulated sugar
- 4 large eggs
- 1 cup (240ml) sour cream
- 1/2 cup (120ml) heavy cream
- 1 teaspoon vanilla extract
- 1 tablespoon lemon zest
- 2 tablespoons all-purpose flour or cornstarch

For the Topping (optional):

- Powdered sugar for dusting
- Fresh berries or fruit preserves for garnish

Instructions:

1. **Prepare the Crust:**
    1. Preheat your oven to 350°F (175°C). Grease a 9-inch (23cm) springform pan.
    2. In a medium bowl, mix the graham cracker crumbs or digestive biscuit crumbs with the sugar. Stir in the melted butter until the mixture resembles wet sand.
    3. Press the crumb mixture evenly into the bottom of the prepared springform pan. Use the back of a spoon or the bottom of a glass to press it down firmly.
    4. Bake the crust for 10 minutes. Remove from the oven and let it cool while you prepare the filling.
2. **Prepare the Filling:**
    1. In a large mixing bowl, combine the quark, sugar, and lemon zest. Mix until smooth.
    2. Add the eggs one at a time, mixing well after each addition.
    3. Stir in the sour cream, heavy cream, and vanilla extract until fully combined.
    4. Add the flour or cornstarch and mix until smooth. This helps to stabilize the filling and prevent cracking.
3. **Bake the Cheesecake:**
    1. Pour the filling into the cooled crust, smoothing the top with a spatula.

2. Bake in the preheated oven for 55-65 minutes, or until the center is set and the edges are lightly golden. The center should still be slightly jiggly; it will firm up as it cools.
3. Turn off the oven and let the cheesecake cool in the oven with the door slightly ajar for about 1 hour. This helps to prevent cracking.

4. **Chill the Cheesecake:**
    1. After the cake has cooled, cover it and refrigerate for at least 4 hours, or overnight, to let it fully set and develop its flavors.
5. **Serve:**
    1. Before serving, you can dust the top with powdered sugar and garnish with fresh berries or fruit preserves if desired.
    2. Run a knife around the edges of the springform pan to loosen the cheesecake, then remove the sides of the pan.

Enjoy this creamy, light, and flavorful German cheesecake that's perfect for any occasion!

Streuselkuchen (Crumb Cake)

Ingredients:

For the Cake:

- 2 1/2 cups (315g) all-purpose flour
- 1 cup (200g) granulated sugar
- 1/2 cup (115g) unsalted butter, softened
- 1 cup (240ml) milk
- 2 large eggs
- 1 tablespoon baking powder
- 1/4 teaspoon salt
- 1 teaspoon vanilla extract

For the Streusel Topping:

- 1 cup (125g) all-purpose flour
- 1/2 cup (100g) granulated sugar
- 1/2 cup (115g) unsalted butter, cold and cubed
- 1 teaspoon ground cinnamon (optional)

For Garnish (optional):

- Powdered sugar for dusting

Instructions:

1. **Prepare the Cake:**
    1. Preheat your oven to 350°F (175°C). Grease and flour a 9-inch (23cm) round cake pan or a 9x13-inch (23x33cm) baking dish.
    2. In a large mixing bowl, cream together the softened butter and granulated sugar until light and fluffy.
    3. Beat in the eggs, one at a time, then stir in the vanilla extract.
    4. In another bowl, whisk together the flour, baking powder, and salt.
    5. Gradually add the dry ingredients to the butter mixture, alternating with the milk, beginning and ending with the dry ingredients. Mix until just combined.
    6. Pour the batter into the prepared pan and smooth the top with a spatula.
2. **Prepare the Streusel Topping:**
    1. In a medium bowl, combine the flour, sugar, and ground cinnamon (if using).
    2. Add the cold, cubed butter. Using your fingers or a pastry cutter, mix until the mixture resembles coarse crumbs.
3. **Assemble the Cake:**
    1. Sprinkle the streusel topping evenly over the cake batter in the pan.
    2. Bake in the preheated oven for 35-45 minutes, or until a toothpick inserted into the center of the cake comes out clean and the topping is golden brown.

4. **Cool and Serve:**
    1. Allow the cake to cool in the pan on a wire rack.
    2. If desired, dust with powdered sugar before serving.

Enjoy this delightful crumb cake with a cup of coffee or tea, or simply as a sweet treat any time of day!

Apfelstrudel (Apple Strudel)

Ingredients:

For the Dough:

- 1 1/2 cups (190g) all-purpose flour
- 1/4 teaspoon salt
- 1/2 teaspoon granulated sugar
- 1/2 cup (115g) unsalted butter, softened
- 1/4 cup (60ml) warm water
- 1 large egg

For the Filling:

- 6 medium apples (such as Granny Smith or a mix of tart and sweet apples), peeled, cored, and thinly sliced
- 1/2 cup (100g) granulated sugar
- 1/2 teaspoon ground cinnamon
- 1/4 teaspoon ground nutmeg
- 1 tablespoon lemon juice
- 1/2 cup (50g) raisins or sultanas (optional)
- 1/2 cup (50g) chopped walnuts or almonds (optional)
- 1/2 cup (60g) fresh bread crumbs or crushed digestive biscuits
- 2 tablespoons unsalted butter, melted

For the Topping:

- 1 egg, beaten (for egg wash)
- Powdered sugar, for dusting

Instructions:

1. **Prepare the Dough:**
    1. In a large bowl, combine the flour, salt, and sugar. Cut in the softened butter until the mixture resembles coarse crumbs.
    2. In a separate bowl, mix the warm water and egg. Add this mixture to the flour mixture and stir until a dough forms.
    3. Transfer the dough to a lightly floured surface and knead for about 5 minutes, or until smooth and elastic.
    4. Shape the dough into a ball, cover with plastic wrap, and let it rest for at least 30 minutes at room temperature.
2. **Prepare the Filling:**
    1. In a large bowl, toss the sliced apples with sugar, cinnamon, nutmeg, and lemon juice.
    2. If using, stir in the raisins or sultanas and the chopped nuts.

3. In a small skillet, toast the bread crumbs or crushed biscuits in 2 tablespoons of melted butter over medium heat until golden brown. Let them cool, then stir them into the apple mixture. This helps absorb excess moisture from the apples.

3. **Assemble the Strudel:**
    1. Preheat your oven to 375°F (190°C). Line a baking sheet with parchment paper.
    2. On a lightly floured surface, roll out the dough as thinly as possible into a large rectangle (about 16x12 inches or 40x30 cm). You can also roll it out between two sheets of parchment paper to prevent sticking.
    3. Brush the dough with melted butter. Spread the apple mixture evenly over the dough, leaving a small border around the edges.
    4. Carefully lift one edge of the dough and begin rolling it up, like a jelly roll, to enclose the filling. Pinch the ends and seams to seal.
    5. Transfer the rolled strudel to the prepared baking sheet, seam side down. Brush with the beaten egg.
4. **Bake the Strudel:**
    1. Bake in the preheated oven for 35-45 minutes, or until the strudel is golden brown and the filling is bubbling.
    2. Remove from the oven and let it cool slightly on a wire rack.
5. **Serve:**
    1. Dust the cooled strudel with powdered sugar before serving.
    2. Slice and serve warm, ideally with a scoop of vanilla ice cream or a dollop of whipped cream.

Enjoy this classic and comforting pastry that's perfect for any occasion!

Zitronenkuchen (Lemon Cake)

Ingredients:

For the Cake:

- 1 1/2 cups (190g) all-purpose flour
- 1 1/2 teaspoons baking powder
- 1/4 teaspoon salt
- 1/2 cup (115g) unsalted butter, softened
- 1 cup (200g) granulated sugar
- 2 large eggs
- 1/2 cup (120ml) milk
- 1/4 cup (60ml) fresh lemon juice (about 1-2 lemons)
- Zest of 1 lemon
- 1 teaspoon vanilla extract

For the Lemon Glaze:

- 1 cup (120g) powdered sugar
- 2-3 tablespoons fresh lemon juice

Instructions:

1. **Prepare the Cake:**
    1. Preheat your oven to 350°F (175°C). Grease and flour a 9-inch round cake pan or a loaf pan.
    2. In a medium bowl, whisk together the flour, baking powder, and salt. Set aside.
    3. In a large bowl, beat the softened butter and granulated sugar together until light and fluffy.
    4. Add the eggs one at a time, beating well after each addition. Mix in the vanilla extract.
    5. Gradually add the dry ingredients to the butter mixture, alternating with the milk, beginning and ending with the dry ingredients. Mix until just combined.
    6. Stir in the lemon juice and lemon zest until evenly distributed.
    7. Pour the batter into the prepared pan and smooth the top with a spatula.
    8. Bake in the preheated oven for 25-30 minutes, or until a toothpick inserted into the center comes out clean. If using a loaf pan, baking time may be closer to 45-50 minutes.
2. **Prepare the Lemon Glaze:**
    1. In a small bowl, whisk together the powdered sugar and lemon juice until smooth. Adjust the consistency by adding more lemon juice if needed to reach your desired thickness.
3. **Finish the Cake:**

    1. Let the cake cool in the pan for about 10 minutes, then transfer it to a wire rack to cool completely.
    2. Once the cake is completely cool, drizzle the lemon glaze over the top. Allow the glaze to set before serving.
4. **Serve:**
    1. Slice and serve the lemon cake. It pairs wonderfully with a cup of tea or coffee.

Enjoy this zesty, moist lemon cake that's perfect for brightening up any day!

Gugelhupf (Bundt Cake)

Ingredients:

For the Cake:

- 2 1/2 cups (315g) all-purpose flour
- 1 1/2 teaspoons baking powder
- 1/4 teaspoon salt
- 1 cup (225g) unsalted butter, softened
- 1 1/2 cups (300g) granulated sugar
- 4 large eggs
- 1 cup (240ml) milk
- 1 teaspoon vanilla extract
- Zest of 1 lemon or orange (optional, for added flavor)

For the Glaze (optional):

- 1 cup (120g) powdered sugar
- 2-3 tablespoons milk or lemon juice
- 1/2 teaspoon vanilla extract

For the Pan:

- 1-2 tablespoons unsalted butter, for greasing
- 1/4 cup (30g) all-purpose flour, for dusting

Instructions:

1. **Prepare the Pan:**
    1. Preheat your oven to 350°F (175°C).
    2. Generously grease the Bundt pan with butter, making sure to get into all the crevices. Dust with flour, tapping out any excess. Alternatively, you can use a non-stick spray with flour.
2. **Prepare the Cake Batter:**
    1. In a medium bowl, whisk together the flour, baking powder, and salt. Set aside.
    2. In a large bowl, beat the softened butter and granulated sugar together until light and fluffy.
    3. Add the eggs one at a time, beating well after each addition. Mix in the vanilla extract (and lemon or orange zest, if using).
    4. Gradually add the dry ingredients to the butter mixture, alternating with the milk, beginning and ending with the dry ingredients. Mix until just combined.
3. **Bake the Cake:**
    1. Pour the batter into the prepared Bundt pan and smooth the top with a spatula.
    2. Bake in the preheated oven for 45-55 minutes, or until a toothpick inserted into the center comes out clean and the cake springs back when lightly pressed.

3. Let the cake cool in the pan for about 15 minutes, then carefully invert it onto a wire rack to cool completely.
4. **Prepare the Glaze (if using):**
    1. In a small bowl, whisk together the powdered sugar, milk or lemon juice, and vanilla extract until smooth. Adjust the consistency by adding more milk or powdered sugar if needed.
    2. Drizzle the glaze over the cooled cake, allowing it to drip down the sides.
5. **Serve:**
    1. Slice and serve the Gugelhupf. It's perfect with a cup of tea or coffee.

Enjoy this classic and versatile cake that can be adapted with various flavors and additions like nuts, chocolate chips, or dried fruits!

Rhabarberkuchen (Rhubarb Cake)

Ingredients:

For the Cake:

- 1 1/2 cups (190g) all-purpose flour
- 1 1/2 teaspoons baking powder
- 1/4 teaspoon salt
- 1/2 cup (115g) unsalted butter, softened
- 1 cup (200g) granulated sugar
- 2 large eggs
- 1 teaspoon vanilla extract
- 1/2 cup (120ml) milk

For the Rhubarb Topping:

- 3 cups (350g) rhubarb stalks, trimmed and cut into 1/2-inch pieces
- 1/2 cup (100g) granulated sugar
- 1 tablespoon all-purpose flour

For the Streusel Topping (optional):

- 1/2 cup (65g) all-purpose flour
- 1/4 cup (50g) granulated sugar
- 1/4 cup (60g) unsalted butter, cold and cubed
- 1/2 teaspoon ground cinnamon (optional)

For Garnish (optional):

- Powdered sugar for dusting

Instructions:

1. **Prepare the Cake:**
    1. Preheat your oven to 350°F (175°C). Grease and flour a 9-inch square or round baking pan.
    2. In a medium bowl, whisk together the flour, baking powder, and salt. Set aside.
    3. In a large bowl, cream together the softened butter and granulated sugar until light and fluffy.
    4. Beat in the eggs one at a time, then mix in the vanilla extract.
    5. Gradually add the dry ingredients to the butter mixture, alternating with the milk, beginning and ending with the dry ingredients. Mix until just combined.
    6. Spread the batter evenly in the prepared pan.
2. **Prepare the Rhubarb Topping:**

1. In a medium bowl, toss the rhubarb pieces with the sugar and flour. This helps to thicken the rhubarb juice and sweeten it.
3. **Prepare the Streusel Topping (if using):**
    1. In a small bowl, mix the flour, sugar, and cinnamon. Add the cold, cubed butter and use your fingers or a pastry cutter to blend until the mixture resembles coarse crumbs.
4. **Assemble the Cake:**
    1. Evenly distribute the rhubarb topping over the cake batter. If using, sprinkle the streusel topping over the rhubarb.
5. **Bake the Cake:**
    1. Bake in the preheated oven for 35-45 minutes, or until a toothpick inserted into the center comes out clean and the rhubarb is tender.
    2. Let the cake cool in the pan on a wire rack.
6. **Serve:**
    1. Dust with powdered sugar if desired before serving.
    2. Slice and enjoy this delightful cake as a sweet treat or a light dessert.

This Rhubarb Cake combines the tartness of rhubarb with a tender cake base and optionally, a crumbly streusel topping for added texture and flavor. Enjoy this classic and refreshing cake!

Nusstorte (Nut Cake)

Ingredients:

For the Cake:

- 1 cup (120g) all-purpose flour
- 1 teaspoon baking powder
- 1/4 teaspoon salt
- 1/2 cup (115g) unsalted butter, softened
- 1 cup (200g) granulated sugar
- 3 large eggs
- 1 teaspoon vanilla extract
- 1 cup (100g) finely chopped nuts (walnuts or hazelnuts)

For the Nut Filling:

- 1 cup (100g) finely chopped nuts (walnuts or hazelnuts)
- 1/2 cup (100g) granulated sugar
- 1/2 cup (120ml) heavy cream

For the Ganache (optional):

- 1/2 cup (120ml) heavy cream
- 4 oz (115g) bittersweet or semisweet chocolate, chopped

For Garnish (optional):

- Whole nuts for decoration

Instructions:

1. **Prepare the Cake:**
    1. Preheat your oven to 350°F (175°C). Grease and flour an 8-inch round cake pan or line it with parchment paper.
    2. In a medium bowl, whisk together the flour, baking powder, and salt. Set aside.
    3. In a large bowl, cream together the softened butter and granulated sugar until light and fluffy.
    4. Add the eggs one at a time, beating well after each addition. Mix in the vanilla extract.
    5. Gradually add the dry ingredients to the butter mixture, mixing until just combined. Fold in the finely chopped nuts.
    6. Pour the batter into the prepared cake pan and smooth the top with a spatula.
    7. Bake in the preheated oven for 25-30 minutes, or until a toothpick inserted into the center comes out clean. Let the cake cool in the pan for 10 minutes, then turn out onto a wire rack to cool completely.

2. **Prepare the Nut Filling:**
    1. In a medium saucepan, combine the finely chopped nuts, granulated sugar, and heavy cream.
    2. Cook over medium heat, stirring constantly, until the mixture thickens and becomes a caramel-like consistency (about 5-7 minutes).
    3. Allow the filling to cool slightly before spreading it on the cooled cake.
3. **Prepare the Ganache (if using):**
    1. In a small saucepan, heat the heavy cream until just simmering.
    2. Pour the hot cream over the chopped chocolate in a heatproof bowl. Let it sit for a few minutes, then stir until smooth and glossy.
    3. Let the ganache cool slightly before spreading it over the nut filling on the cake.
4. **Assemble the Cake:**
    1. Spread the nut filling evenly over the top of the cooled cake.
    2. If using ganache, spread it evenly over the nut filling.
5. **Garnish and Serve:**
    1. Decorate with whole nuts if desired.
    2. Slice and serve. The cake can be stored in an airtight container at room temperature for a few days or in the refrigerator for longer shelf life.

Enjoy this rich and nutty cake that's sure to impress at any gathering!

Linzer Torte

Ingredients:

For the Dough:

- 1 1/2 cups (180g) all-purpose flour
- 1 cup (100g) finely ground almonds (or hazelnuts)
- 1/2 cup (100g) granulated sugar
- 1/2 teaspoon ground cinnamon
- 1/4 teaspoon ground cloves
- 1/4 teaspoon salt
- 1/2 cup (115g) unsalted butter, cold and cut into small pieces
- 1 large egg
- 1 teaspoon vanilla extract

For the Filling:

- 1 cup (300g) raspberry jam (or apricot jam, for a different variation)
- 1 tablespoon lemon juice (optional, for added brightness)

For the Decoration:

- Powdered sugar, for dusting (optional)

Instructions:

1. **Prepare the Dough:**
    1. In a large bowl, whisk together the flour, ground almonds, sugar, cinnamon, cloves, and salt.
    2. Add the cold butter pieces and use a pastry cutter or your fingers to cut the butter into the dry ingredients until the mixture resembles coarse crumbs.
    3. In a small bowl, beat the egg with the vanilla extract, then add it to the flour mixture. Mix until the dough begins to come together.
    4. Gather the dough into a ball, flatten it into a disk, wrap it in plastic wrap, and refrigerate for at least 30 minutes.
2. **Preheat the Oven:**
    1. Preheat your oven to 350°F (175°C). Grease and flour a 9-inch (23cm) tart pan with a removable bottom.
3. **Roll Out the Dough:**
    1. On a lightly floured surface, roll out about 2/3 of the dough to fit the bottom of the tart pan. Carefully transfer the dough to the pan, pressing it evenly into the bottom and up the sides. Trim any excess dough from the edges.
    2. Spread the raspberry jam evenly over the dough. If desired, mix the lemon juice into the jam for a touch of acidity.
4. **Make the Lattice:**

1. Roll out the remaining dough on a floured surface. Cut it into strips (about 1/2-inch wide) to create a lattice pattern over the jam filling.
   2. Arrange the strips in a lattice pattern over the jam. Press the edges to seal them to the crust.
5. **Bake the Torte:**
   1. Bake in the preheated oven for 35-45 minutes, or until the crust is golden brown and the jam is bubbly.
   2. Remove from the oven and let the torte cool completely in the pan on a wire rack.
6. **Serve:**
   1. Once cooled, remove the torte from the pan. Dust with powdered sugar if desired before serving.
   2. Slice and enjoy with a cup of tea or coffee.

This Linzer Torte offers a delightful combination of flavors and textures, with its buttery crust, nutty undertones, and sweet, tangy jam filling. It's perfect for special occasions or as a treat any time of year!

Marzipan Torte

Ingredients:

For the Cake:

- 1 1/2 cups (190g) all-purpose flour
- 1 1/2 teaspoons baking powder
- 1/4 teaspoon salt
- 1/2 cup (115g) unsalted butter, softened
- 1 cup (200g) granulated sugar
- 4 large eggs
- 1 teaspoon vanilla extract
- 1/2 cup (120ml) milk

For the Filling:

- 1 cup (240ml) heavy cream
- 2 tablespoons powdered sugar
- 1 teaspoon vanilla extract

For the Marzipan Layer:

- 8 oz (225g) marzipan, rolled out to 1/8-inch thickness
- 1/4 cup (60ml) apricot jam or preserves

For the Decoration:

- Powdered sugar for dusting
- Optional: Fresh fruit or edible flowers for garnish

Instructions:

1. **Prepare the Cake:**
    1. Preheat your oven to 350°F (175°C). Grease and flour a 9-inch round cake pan or line it with parchment paper.
    2. In a medium bowl, whisk together the flour, baking powder, and salt. Set aside.
    3. In a large bowl, cream together the softened butter and granulated sugar until light and fluffy.
    4. Beat in the eggs one at a time, mixing well after each addition. Stir in the vanilla extract.
    5. Gradually add the dry ingredients to the butter mixture, alternating with the milk, beginning and ending with the dry ingredients. Mix until just combined.
    6. Pour the batter into the prepared pan and smooth the top with a spatula.

7. Bake in the preheated oven for 25-30 minutes, or until a toothpick inserted into the center comes out clean. Let the cake cool in the pan for 10 minutes, then turn out onto a wire rack to cool completely.

2. **Prepare the Filling:**
   1. In a medium bowl, whip the heavy cream with the powdered sugar and vanilla extract until stiff peaks form.
3. **Prepare the Marzipan Layer:**
   1. Roll out the marzipan on a lightly powdered sugar-dusted surface to about 1/8-inch thickness. Ensure it's large enough to cover the top of the cake.
   2. Heat the apricot jam in a small saucepan over low heat until it becomes liquid. Strain it if there are pieces of fruit.
4. **Assemble the Cake:**
   1. If the cake has domed slightly, level the top with a knife.
   2. Spread the whipped cream evenly over the top and sides of the cooled cake.
   3. Brush the top of the cake with a thin layer of apricot jam.
   4. Carefully place the rolled-out marzipan over the cake, smoothing it down and trimming any excess around the edges.
5. **Decorate the Cake:**
   1. Dust the top of the marzipan with powdered sugar if desired.
   2. Garnish with fresh fruit, edible flowers, or any other decoration of your choice.
6. **Serve:**
   1. Slice and serve the Marzipan Torte. It pairs beautifully with a cup of tea or coffee.

This Marzipan Torte combines the nutty sweetness of marzipan with a light sponge cake and a luscious cream filling, making it a decadent and delightful treat for any occasion.

Joghurtkuchen (Yogurt Cake)

Ingredients:

For the Cake:

- 1 cup (240ml) plain yogurt (full-fat or low-fat)
- 1 cup (200g) granulated sugar
- 1/2 cup (115g) unsalted butter, melted and cooled
- 3 large eggs
- 1 1/2 cups (190g) all-purpose flour
- 1 1/2 teaspoons baking powder
- 1/2 teaspoon baking soda
- 1/4 teaspoon salt
- 1 teaspoon vanilla extract
- Zest of 1 lemon (optional, for added flavor)

For the Glaze (optional):

- 1/2 cup (60g) powdered sugar
- 2-3 tablespoons lemon juice or milk

For Garnish (optional):

- Fresh berries or a dusting of powdered sugar

Instructions:

1. **Prepare the Cake:**
    1. Preheat your oven to 350°F (175°C). Grease and flour an 8-inch round cake pan or a 9x9-inch square baking pan.
    2. In a large bowl, whisk together the yogurt, granulated sugar, melted butter, and eggs until well combined.
    3. In a separate bowl, sift together the flour, baking powder, baking soda, and salt.
    4. Gradually add the dry ingredients to the wet ingredients, mixing until just combined. Stir in the vanilla extract and lemon zest if using.
    5. Pour the batter into the prepared pan and smooth the top with a spatula.
2. **Bake the Cake:**
    1. Bake in the preheated oven for 30-40 minutes, or until a toothpick inserted into the center comes out clean and the top is golden brown.
    2. Let the cake cool in the pan for 10 minutes, then transfer it to a wire rack to cool completely.
3. **Prepare the Glaze (if using):**
    1. In a small bowl, whisk together the powdered sugar and lemon juice or milk until smooth. Adjust the consistency by adding more liquid or powdered sugar if needed.

4. **Serve:**
    1. Once the cake is completely cool, drizzle the glaze over the top if desired.
    2. Garnish with fresh berries or a dusting of powdered sugar if you like.

This Joghurtkuchen is light, moist, and incredibly easy to make. It's perfect for breakfast, a snack, or a light dessert. Enjoy!

Karpatka (Carpathian Cake)

Ingredients:

For the Dough:

- 1 cup (230ml) water
- 1/2 cup (115g) unsalted butter
- 1 cup (130g) all-purpose flour
- 4 large eggs

For the Filling:

- 2 cups (480ml) milk
- 1 cup (200g) granulated sugar
- 1/2 cup (100g) granulated sugar
- 1/4 cup (30g) all-purpose flour
- 1/4 cup (30g) cornstarch
- 1 teaspoon vanilla extract
- 1/4 cup (60g) unsalted butter

For Dusting (optional):

- Powdered sugar

Instructions:

1. **Prepare the Dough:**
    1. Preheat your oven to 400°F (200°C). Line two baking sheets with parchment paper.
    2. In a medium saucepan, bring the water and butter to a boil over medium heat.
    3. Once the butter has melted, remove the pan from heat and quickly stir in the flour all at once, mixing until the dough forms a ball and pulls away from the sides of the pan.
    4. Allow the dough to cool slightly, then beat in the eggs one at a time, making sure each egg is fully incorporated before adding the next. The dough should be smooth and glossy.
    5. Divide the dough evenly between the two prepared baking sheets, spreading it into an even layer.
2. **Bake the Dough:**
    1. Bake in the preheated oven for 20-25 minutes, or until the dough is golden brown and puffed.
    2. Remove from the oven and let the pastry cool on the baking sheets for a few minutes before transferring to a wire rack to cool completely.
3. **Prepare the Filling:**

1. In a medium saucepan, heat the milk until it is just about to boil. In a separate bowl, whisk together the sugar, flour, and cornstarch.
2. Gradually whisk the sugar mixture into the hot milk. Continue to cook over medium heat, whisking constantly, until the mixture thickens and comes to a boil.
3. Remove from heat and stir in the vanilla extract and butter. Let the custard cool to room temperature, stirring occasionally to prevent a skin from forming.

4. **Assemble the Cake:**
    1. Once the pastry layers and custard are completely cool, spread the custard evenly over one of the pastry layers.
    2. Place the second pastry layer on top of the custard, pressing gently to adhere.
5. **Serve:**
    1. Dust the top with powdered sugar if desired.
    2. Slice and serve. The cake is best enjoyed after chilling in the refrigerator for a few hours to let the flavors meld.

This Karpatka offers a delightful combination of crisp pastry and creamy custard, making it a memorable dessert for any occasion. Enjoy this traditional treat!

Zwetschgenkuchen (Plum Cake)

Ingredients:

For the Dough:

- 1 1/2 cups (190g) all-purpose flour
- 1/2 cup (100g) granulated sugar
- 1/2 cup (115g) unsalted butter, cold and cut into small pieces
- 1 large egg
- 1 teaspoon baking powder
- 1/4 teaspoon salt

For the Plum Topping:

- 2 lbs (900g) plums, pitted and sliced (Zwetschgen or Italian plums are ideal)
- 1/4 cup (50g) granulated sugar
- 1 teaspoon ground cinnamon
- 1 tablespoon lemon juice (optional, for added flavor)

For the Streusel Topping (optional but recommended):

- 1/2 cup (65g) all-purpose flour
- 1/4 cup (50g) granulated sugar
- 1/4 cup (60g) unsalted butter, cold and cut into small pieces
- 1/2 teaspoon ground cinnamon (optional)

Instructions:

1. **Prepare the Dough:**
    1. Preheat your oven to 350°F (175°C). Grease and flour a 9-inch round cake pan or a 9x13-inch baking pan.
    2. In a medium bowl, mix the flour, sugar, baking powder, and salt.
    3. Cut in the cold butter using a pastry cutter or your fingers until the mixture resembles coarse crumbs.
    4. Beat the egg and add it to the flour mixture. Mix until just combined. The dough should come together but will be slightly crumbly.
    5. Press the dough evenly into the bottom of the prepared pan to form the base.
2. **Prepare the Plum Topping:**
    1. In a large bowl, toss the plum slices with sugar, cinnamon, and lemon juice if using.
3. **Assemble the Cake:**
    1. Arrange the plum slices evenly over the dough in the pan.
4. **Prepare the Streusel Topping (if using):**
    1. In a small bowl, mix the flour, sugar, and cinnamon.
    2. Cut in the cold butter until the mixture resembles coarse crumbs.

    3. Sprinkle the streusel evenly over the plums.
5. **Bake the Cake:**
    1. Bake in the preheated oven for 40-50 minutes, or until the cake is golden brown and the plums are tender.
    2. Allow the cake to cool in the pan for about 10 minutes before transferring it to a wire rack to cool completely.
6. **Serve:**
    1. Slice and serve the Zwetschgenkuchen warm or at room temperature. It's delightful on its own or with a dollop of whipped cream or a scoop of vanilla ice cream.

This Zwetschgenkuchen is a delicious way to enjoy plums, with a tender base and a flavorful, slightly spiced topping. Perfect for a cozy dessert or a special occasion!

Donauwelle (Danube Wave Cake)

Ingredients:

For the Cake:

- 1 1/2 cups (190g) all-purpose flour
- 1 1/2 teaspoons baking powder
- 1/4 teaspoon salt
- 1 cup (225g) unsalted butter, softened
- 1 cup (200g) granulated sugar
- 4 large eggs
- 1 teaspoon vanilla extract
- 1/2 cup (120ml) milk
- 1/4 cup (25g) unsweetened cocoa powder
- 1/4 cup (60ml) hot water

For the Cherry Layer:

- 1 can (14 oz/400g) sour cherries, drained and pitted (or use fresh, pitted cherries if available)
- 2 tablespoons granulated sugar

For the Buttercream:

- 1 cup (225g) unsalted butter, softened
- 2 cups (240g) powdered sugar
- 2 tablespoons milk
- 1 teaspoon vanilla extract

For the Chocolate Glaze:

- 4 oz (115g) bittersweet or semisweet chocolate, chopped
- 1/4 cup (60ml) heavy cream

Instructions:

1. **Prepare the Cake:**
    1. Preheat your oven to 350°F (175°C). Grease and flour a 9x13-inch baking pan.
    2. In a medium bowl, whisk together the flour, baking powder, and salt. Set aside.
    3. In a large bowl, cream together the softened butter and granulated sugar until light and fluffy.
    4. Beat in the eggs one at a time, mixing well after each addition. Stir in the vanilla extract.
    5. Gradually add the dry ingredients to the butter mixture, alternating with the milk, beginning and ending with the dry ingredients. Mix until just combined.

6. In a small bowl, mix the cocoa powder with the hot water to make a smooth chocolate paste.
7. Divide the batter in half. Mix the chocolate paste into one half of the batter.

2. **Assemble the Cake:**
    1. Spoon alternating dollops of vanilla and chocolate batter into the prepared pan. Use a knife or skewer to swirl the batters together to create a marble effect.
    2. Bake in the preheated oven for 30-35 minutes, or until a toothpick inserted into the center comes out clean. Allow the cake to cool completely in the pan on a wire rack.
3. **Prepare the Cherry Layer:**
    1. Toss the sour cherries with the granulated sugar. Once the cake is completely cooled, spread the cherries evenly over the cake.
4. **Prepare the Buttercream:**
    1. In a large bowl, beat the softened butter until creamy. Gradually add the powdered sugar, milk, and vanilla extract. Beat until smooth and fluffy.
    2. Spread the buttercream evenly over the cherry layer.
5. **Prepare the Chocolate Glaze:**
    1. In a small saucepan, heat the heavy cream until just simmering. Remove from heat and add the chopped chocolate. Let it sit for a minute, then stir until smooth.
    2. Allow the glaze to cool slightly before spreading it over the buttercream layer.
6. **Serve:**
    1. Let the glaze set before cutting the cake into squares or rectangles.
    2. Serve and enjoy!

Donauwelle is a show-stopping dessert with its beautiful marble cake, tart cherries, creamy buttercream, and glossy chocolate glaze. It's perfect for special occasions or as a delightful treat any time!

Kaffekuchen (Coffee Cake)

Ingredients:

For the Cake:

- 1 1/2 cups (190g) all-purpose flour
- 1 cup (200g) granulated sugar
- 1/2 cup (115g) unsalted butter, softened
- 1/2 cup (120ml) milk
- 2 large eggs
- 1 1/2 teaspoons baking powder
- 1/4 teaspoon baking soda
- 1/4 teaspoon salt
- 1 teaspoon vanilla extract

For the Cinnamon-Sugar Swirl:

- 1/2 cup (100g) granulated sugar
- 1 tablespoon ground cinnamon

For the Streusel Topping:

- 1/2 cup (65g) all-purpose flour
- 1/4 cup (50g) granulated sugar
- 1/4 cup (60g) unsalted butter, cold and cut into small pieces
- 1/2 teaspoon ground cinnamon

Instructions:

1. **Preheat the Oven:**
    1. Preheat your oven to 350°F (175°C). Grease and flour a 9-inch round cake pan or a 9x9-inch square baking pan.
2. **Prepare the Cinnamon-Sugar Swirl:**
    1. In a small bowl, mix together the granulated sugar and ground cinnamon. Set aside.
3. **Prepare the Streusel Topping:**
    1. In another small bowl, combine the flour, sugar, and cinnamon.
    2. Cut in the cold butter using a pastry cutter or your fingers until the mixture resembles coarse crumbs. Set aside.
4. **Prepare the Cake Batter:**
    1. In a medium bowl, whisk together the flour, baking powder, baking soda, and salt. Set aside.
    2. In a large bowl, cream together the softened butter and granulated sugar until light and fluffy.

3. Beat in the eggs one at a time, mixing well after each addition. Stir in the vanilla extract.
4. Gradually add the dry ingredients to the butter mixture, alternating with the milk, beginning and ending with the dry ingredients. Mix until just combined.

5. **Assemble the Cake:**
   1. Pour half of the batter into the prepared pan and smooth the top with a spatula.
   2. Sprinkle half of the cinnamon-sugar mixture evenly over the batter.
   3. Spoon the remaining batter over the cinnamon-sugar layer and spread evenly.
   4. Sprinkle the remaining cinnamon-sugar mixture over the top.
   5. Scatter the streusel topping evenly over the batter.

6. **Bake the Cake:**
   1. Bake in the preheated oven for 35-45 minutes, or until a toothpick inserted into the center comes out clean and the top is golden brown.
   2. Allow the cake to cool in the pan for 10 minutes before transferring to a wire rack to cool completely.

7. **Serve:**
   1. Slice and serve the Kaffekuchen warm or at room temperature. It's perfect for enjoying with a cup of coffee or tea.

This Kaffekuchen is a simple yet satisfying treat with its flavorful cinnamon swirl and crumbly streusel topping. It's a great addition to any coffee break or afternoon snack!

Heidelbeerkuchen (Blueberry Cake)

Ingredients:

For the Cake:

- 1 1/2 cups (190g) all-purpose flour
- 1 cup (200g) granulated sugar
- 1/2 cup (115g) unsalted butter, softened
- 2 large eggs
- 1/2 cup (120ml) milk
- 1 1/2 teaspoons baking powder
- 1/4 teaspoon salt
- 1 teaspoon vanilla extract
- 1 1/2 cups (225g) fresh or frozen blueberries (if using frozen, do not thaw)

For the Crumble Topping:

- 1/2 cup (65g) all-purpose flour
- 1/4 cup (50g) granulated sugar
- 1/4 cup (60g) unsalted butter, cold and cut into small pieces
- 1/2 teaspoon ground cinnamon (optional)

For the Glaze (optional):

- 1/2 cup (60g) powdered sugar
- 2-3 tablespoons lemon juice or milk

Instructions:

1. **Preheat the Oven:**
   1. Preheat your oven to 350°F (175°C). Grease and flour a 9-inch round cake pan or a 9x9-inch square baking pan. Line with parchment paper for easier removal.
2. **Prepare the Crumble Topping:**
   1. In a small bowl, combine the flour, sugar, and ground cinnamon (if using).
   2. Cut in the cold butter using a pastry cutter or your fingers until the mixture resembles coarse crumbs. Set aside.
3. **Prepare the Cake Batter:**
   1. In a medium bowl, whisk together the flour, baking powder, and salt.
   2. In a large bowl, cream together the softened butter and granulated sugar until light and fluffy.
   3. Beat in the eggs one at a time, mixing well after each addition. Stir in the vanilla extract.
   4. Gradually add the dry ingredients to the butter mixture, alternating with the milk, beginning and ending with the dry ingredients. Mix until just combined.
   5. Gently fold in the blueberries.

4. **Assemble the Cake:**
    1. Pour the batter into the prepared pan and spread it evenly.
    2. Sprinkle the crumble topping evenly over the batter.
5. **Bake the Cake:**
    1. Bake in the preheated oven for 35-45 minutes, or until a toothpick inserted into the center comes out clean and the top is golden brown.
    2. Allow the cake to cool in the pan for 10 minutes before transferring it to a wire rack to cool completely.
6. **Prepare the Glaze (if using):**
    1. In a small bowl, whisk together the powdered sugar and lemon juice or milk until smooth. Adjust the consistency with more liquid or powdered sugar if needed.
7. **Serve:**
    1. Once the cake has cooled, drizzle the glaze over the top if desired.
    2. Slice and serve. Enjoy this cake with a cup of coffee or tea!

Heidelbeerkuchen is a delightful way to enjoy fresh or frozen blueberries, with its tender crumb and crunchy crumble topping. It's a perfect treat for any time of year!

Apfelkuchen (Apple Cake)

Ingredients:

For the Cake:

- 1 1/2 cups (190g) all-purpose flour
- 1 cup (200g) granulated sugar
- 1/2 cup (115g) unsalted butter, softened
- 2 large eggs
- 1/2 cup (120ml) milk
- 1 1/2 teaspoons baking powder
- 1/4 teaspoon baking soda
- 1/4 teaspoon salt
- 1 teaspoon vanilla extract
- 3-4 medium apples, peeled, cored, and thinly sliced (about 2 cups or 300g)

For the Apple Spice Mixture:

- 1/4 cup (50g) granulated sugar
- 1 teaspoon ground cinnamon
- 1/4 teaspoon ground nutmeg (optional)

For the Streusel Topping (optional):

- 1/2 cup (65g) all-purpose flour
- 1/4 cup (50g) granulated sugar
- 1/4 cup (60g) unsalted butter, cold and cut into small pieces
- 1/2 teaspoon ground cinnamon

Instructions:

1. **Preheat the Oven:**
    1. Preheat your oven to 350°F (175°C). Grease and flour a 9-inch round cake pan or a 9x9-inch square baking pan. Line with parchment paper if desired for easier removal.
2. **Prepare the Apple Spice Mixture:**
    1. In a small bowl, mix together the granulated sugar, ground cinnamon, and ground nutmeg (if using). Set aside.
3. **Prepare the Cake Batter:**
    1. In a medium bowl, whisk together the flour, baking powder, baking soda, and salt.
    2. In a large bowl, cream together the softened butter and granulated sugar until light and fluffy.
    3. Beat in the eggs one at a time, mixing well after each addition. Stir in the vanilla extract.

4. Gradually add the dry ingredients to the butter mixture, alternating with the milk, beginning and ending with the dry ingredients. Mix until just combined.
5. Gently fold in half of the apple slices, reserving the other half for the top.

4. **Assemble the Cake:**
    1. Pour the batter into the prepared pan and smooth the top.
    2. Arrange the remaining apple slices evenly over the top of the batter.
    3. Sprinkle the apple spice mixture evenly over the apples.
5. **Prepare the Streusel Topping (if using):**
    1. In a small bowl, combine the flour, sugar, and ground cinnamon.
    2. Cut in the cold butter until the mixture resembles coarse crumbs.
    3. Sprinkle the streusel topping over the apples.
6. **Bake the Cake:**
    1. Bake in the preheated oven for 40-50 minutes, or until a toothpick inserted into the center comes out clean and the top is golden brown.
    2. Allow the cake to cool in the pan for 10 minutes before transferring to a wire rack to cool completely.
7. **Serve:**
    1. Slice and serve the Apfelkuchen warm or at room temperature. It's delicious on its own or with a dusting of powdered sugar, and pairs wonderfully with a scoop of vanilla ice cream or a dollop of whipped cream.

This Apfelkuchen is a comforting and flavorful cake that makes the most of apples, with a tender crumb and optional streusel topping for extra texture. Enjoy!

Sachertorte

Ingredients:

For the Cake:

- 1 cup (225g) unsalted butter, softened
- 1 cup (200g) granulated sugar
- 6 large eggs, separated
- 1 teaspoon vanilla extract
- 1 cup (130g) all-purpose flour
- 1/2 cup (50g) unsweetened cocoa powder
- 1/4 teaspoon salt
- 1/2 cup (120ml) water

For the Apricot Glaze:

- 1/2 cup (150g) apricot jam or preserves

For the Chocolate Glaze:

- 4 oz (115g) bittersweet or semisweet chocolate, chopped
- 1/2 cup (120ml) heavy cream

For Serving (optional):

- Whipped cream

Instructions:

1. **Prepare the Cake:**
    1. Preheat your oven to 350°F (175°C). Grease and flour an 8-inch round cake pan or line it with parchment paper.
    2. In a large bowl, cream together the softened butter and granulated sugar until light and fluffy.
    3. Beat in the egg yolks one at a time, mixing well after each addition. Stir in the vanilla extract.
    4. In a separate bowl, sift together the flour, cocoa powder, and salt.
    5. Gradually add the dry ingredients to the butter mixture, alternating with the water, beginning and ending with the dry ingredients. Mix until just combined.
    6. In another bowl, beat the egg whites until stiff peaks form. Gently fold the egg whites into the batter, being careful not to deflate them.
    7. Pour the batter into the prepared pan and smooth the top.
    8. Bake in the preheated oven for 25-30 minutes, or until a toothpick inserted into the center comes out clean. Allow the cake to cool in the pan for 10 minutes, then transfer to a wire rack to cool completely.

2. **Prepare the Apricot Glaze:**
    1. While the cake is cooling, warm the apricot jam in a small saucepan over low heat until it becomes liquid and easy to spread.
    2. Strain the jam through a fine sieve to remove any solids if necessary.
3. **Prepare the Chocolate Glaze:**
    1. In a small saucepan, heat the heavy cream until just simmering. Remove from heat and add the chopped chocolate. Let it sit for a minute, then stir until smooth.
    2. Allow the glaze to cool slightly before using.
4. **Assemble the Cake:**
    1. Once the cake is completely cooled, spread a thin layer of apricot glaze evenly over the top and sides of the cake.
    2. Place the cake on a wire rack set over a baking sheet to catch drips. Pour the chocolate glaze over the cake, spreading it evenly with a spatula to cover the top and sides. Allow the glaze to set.
5. **Serve:**
    1. Slice and serve the Sachertorte at room temperature. It's often accompanied by a dollop of whipped cream.

Sachertorte is renowned for its rich chocolate flavor and elegant presentation. The combination of apricot jam and chocolate glaze creates a delicious contrast that makes this cake a standout dessert. Enjoy this classic Austrian treat!

Krapfen (German Doughnuts)

Ingredients:

For the Dough:

- 1 cup (240ml) whole milk
- 1/4 cup (50g) granulated sugar
- 1/4 cup (60g) unsalted butter, softened
- 2 large eggs
- 2 1/4 teaspoons (1 packet) active dry yeast
- 1/2 teaspoon salt
- 3 1/2 - 4 cups (440-500g) all-purpose flour

For the Filling:

- 1 cup (250g) fruit jam or jelly (such as raspberry, apricot, or strawberry)
- 1/2 cup (150g) pastry cream or chocolate ganache (optional)

For Frying:

- Vegetable oil, for frying

For Dusting:

- Powdered sugar

Instructions:

1. **Prepare the Dough:**
    1. Warm the milk to about 110°F (45°C) and dissolve the granulated sugar in it.
    2. Sprinkle the yeast over the milk and let it sit for about 5-10 minutes, until it becomes frothy.
    3. In a large bowl, mix the flour and salt. Make a well in the center and add the yeast mixture, softened butter, and eggs.
    4. Mix until a sticky dough forms. Knead the dough on a floured surface for about 8-10 minutes, or until it becomes smooth and elastic.
    5. Place the dough in a lightly greased bowl, cover with a damp cloth or plastic wrap, and let it rise in a warm place for about 1-1.5 hours, or until doubled in size.
2. **Shape the Krapfen:**
    1. Punch down the dough and turn it out onto a lightly floured surface. Roll out the dough to about 1/2 inch (1.25 cm) thickness.
    2. Use a round cutter (about 2-3 inches in diameter) to cut out circles from the dough.
    3. Place the circles on a parchment-lined baking sheet and cover with a damp cloth. Let them rise for another 30 minutes, or until slightly puffed.

3. **Fry the Krapfen:**
    1. Heat about 2 inches of vegetable oil in a deep fryer or large heavy pot to 350°F (175°C).
    2. Fry the doughnuts in batches, being careful not to overcrowd the pot. Fry for about 1-2 minutes per side, or until golden brown and cooked through.
    3. Use a slotted spoon to transfer the Krapfen to a paper towel-lined plate to drain excess oil.
4. **Fill the Krapfen:**
    1. Once the Krapfen are cool enough to handle, use a piping bag fitted with a small round tip to fill them with fruit jam, pastry cream, or chocolate ganache. You can also use a long, thin pastry tip or even a toothpick to create a small hole for filling.
    2. Dust the filled Krapfen generously with powdered sugar.
5. **Serve:**
    1. Enjoy the Krapfen fresh, while they're still soft and slightly warm, or at room temperature. They are best eaten the day they are made but can be stored in an airtight container for a day or two.

Krapfen are a delightful treat with their soft, fluffy texture and sweet, fruity filling. They make a wonderful addition to any festive occasion or as a special treat anytime!

Birnenkuchen (Pear Cake)

Ingredients:

For the Cake:

- 1 1/2 cups (190g) all-purpose flour
- 1 cup (200g) granulated sugar
- 1/2 cup (115g) unsalted butter, softened
- 2 large eggs
- 1/2 cup (120ml) milk
- 1 1/2 teaspoons baking powder
- 1/4 teaspoon salt
- 1 teaspoon vanilla extract
- 3-4 ripe pears, peeled, cored, and sliced

For the Cinnamon-Sugar Topping (optional):

- 1/4 cup (50g) granulated sugar
- 1 teaspoon ground cinnamon

For the Streusel Topping (optional):

- 1/2 cup (65g) all-purpose flour
- 1/4 cup (50g) granulated sugar
- 1/4 cup (60g) unsalted butter, cold and cut into small pieces
- 1/2 teaspoon ground cinnamon

Instructions:

1. **Preheat the Oven:**
    1. Preheat your oven to 350°F (175°C). Grease and flour a 9-inch round cake pan or a 9x9-inch square baking pan. You can also line the pan with parchment paper for easier removal.
2. **Prepare the Cake Batter:**
    1. In a medium bowl, whisk together the flour, baking powder, and salt. Set aside.
    2. In a large bowl, cream together the softened butter and granulated sugar until light and fluffy.
    3. Beat in the eggs one at a time, mixing well after each addition. Stir in the vanilla extract.
    4. Gradually add the dry ingredients to the butter mixture, alternating with the milk, beginning and ending with the dry ingredients. Mix until just combined.
3. **Assemble the Cake:**
    1. Pour the batter into the prepared pan and spread it evenly.
    2. Arrange the pear slices on top of the batter, slightly overlapping if necessary.
4. **Prepare the Toppings (optional):**
    For the Cinnamon-Sugar Topping:
    1. In a small bowl, mix the granulated sugar and ground cinnamon.
    2. Sprinkle the mixture evenly over the pear slices.

5. **For the Streusel Topping:**
    1. In a small bowl, combine the flour, sugar, and ground cinnamon.
    2. Cut in the cold butter until the mixture resembles coarse crumbs.
    3. Sprinkle the streusel topping evenly over the pear slices.
6. **Bake the Cake:**
    1. Bake in the preheated oven for 35-45 minutes, or until a toothpick inserted into the center comes out clean and the top is golden brown.
    2. Allow the cake to cool in the pan for 10 minutes before transferring it to a wire rack to cool completely.
7. **Serve:**
    1. Slice and serve the Birnenkuchen warm or at room temperature. It's delightful on its own or with a dusting of powdered sugar, and pairs beautifully with a dollop of whipped cream or a scoop of vanilla ice cream.

Birnenkuchen is a charming dessert that highlights the sweet, delicate flavor of pears. Whether you choose to add a cinnamon-sugar topping or a crumbly streusel, it's a versatile and tasty treat perfect for any occasion!

Bienenstich Cupcakes

Ingredients:

For the Cupcakes:

- 1 1/2 cups (190g) all-purpose flour
- 1 cup (200g) granulated sugar
- 1/2 cup (115g) unsalted butter, softened
- 2 large eggs
- 1/2 cup (120ml) milk
- 1 1/2 teaspoons baking powder
- 1/4 teaspoon salt
- 1 teaspoon vanilla extract

For the Honey Almond Topping:

- 1/2 cup (50g) sliced almonds
- 1/4 cup (60ml) honey
- 2 tablespoons unsalted butter
- 1/4 cup (50g) granulated sugar

For the Cream Filling:

- 1 cup (240ml) heavy cream
- 1/4 cup (30g) powdered sugar
- 1 teaspoon vanilla extract

Instructions:

1. **Preheat the Oven:**
    1. Preheat your oven to 350°F (175°C). Line a 12-cup muffin pan with paper liners.
2. **Prepare the Cupcake Batter:**
    1. In a medium bowl, whisk together the flour, baking powder, and salt. Set aside.
    2. In a large bowl, cream together the softened butter and granulated sugar until light and fluffy.
    3. Beat in the eggs one at a time, mixing well after each addition. Stir in the vanilla extract.
    4. Gradually add the dry ingredients to the butter mixture, alternating with the milk, beginning and ending with the dry ingredients. Mix until just combined.
    5. Divide the batter evenly among the cupcake liners, filling each about 2/3 full.
3. **Bake the Cupcakes:**
    1. Bake in the preheated oven for 18-22 minutes, or until a toothpick inserted into the center comes out clean. Allow the cupcakes to cool in the pan for 5 minutes, then transfer to a wire rack to cool completely.
4. **Prepare the Honey Almond Topping:**
    1. In a small saucepan, melt the butter over medium heat. Stir in the sugar and honey until the sugar is dissolved and the mixture is smooth.

       2. Add the sliced almonds and cook, stirring constantly, until the almonds are golden brown and caramelized, about 3-4 minutes.
       3. Remove from heat and let it cool slightly.
   5. **Prepare the Cream Filling:**
       1. In a medium bowl, whip the heavy cream, powdered sugar, and vanilla extract until stiff peaks form.
   6. **Assemble the Cupcakes:**
       1. Once the cupcakes are completely cool, use a small knife or a cupcake corer to make a small hole in the center of each cupcake.
       2. Fill the hole with the whipped cream, either by spooning it in or using a piping bag.
       3. Spoon or drizzle the honey almond topping over each filled cupcake.
   7. **Serve:**
       1. Serve the Bienenstich Cupcakes immediately or store in an airtight container for up to 2 days.

These Bienenstich Cupcakes bring the classic flavors of the German Bee Sting Cake into a convenient, individual-sized treat, making them perfect for sharing or special occasions. Enjoy the combination of sweet honey, crunchy almonds, and creamy filling!

Himbeerkuchen (Raspberry Cake)

Ingredients:

For the Cake:

- 1 1/2 cups (190g) all-purpose flour
- 1 cup (200g) granulated sugar
- 1/2 cup (115g) unsalted butter, softened
- 2 large eggs
- 1/2 cup (120ml) milk
- 1 1/2 teaspoons baking powder
- 1/4 teaspoon salt
- 1 teaspoon vanilla extract
- 1 1/2 cups (225g) fresh or frozen raspberries (if using frozen, do not thaw)

For the Streusel Topping (optional):

- 1/2 cup (65g) all-purpose flour
- 1/4 cup (50g) granulated sugar
- 1/4 cup (60g) unsalted butter, cold and cut into small pieces
- 1/2 teaspoon ground cinnamon

For the Glaze (optional):

- 1/2 cup (60g) powdered sugar
- 2-3 tablespoons lemon juice or milk

Instructions:

1. **Preheat the Oven:**
    1. Preheat your oven to 350°F (175°C). Grease and flour a 9-inch round cake pan or a 9x9-inch square baking pan. You can also line the pan with parchment paper for easier removal.
2. **Prepare the Streusel Topping (if using):**
    1. In a small bowl, combine the flour, sugar, and ground cinnamon.
    2. Cut in the cold butter using a pastry cutter or your fingers until the mixture resembles coarse crumbs. Set aside.
3. **Prepare the Cake Batter:**
    1. In a medium bowl, whisk together the flour, baking powder, and salt. Set aside.
    2. In a large bowl, cream together the softened butter and granulated sugar until light and fluffy.
    3. Beat in the eggs one at a time, mixing well after each addition. Stir in the vanilla extract.
    4. Gradually add the dry ingredients to the butter mixture, alternating with the milk, beginning and ending with the dry ingredients. Mix until just combined.
    5. Gently fold in the raspberries, being careful not to break them up too much.
4. **Assemble the Cake:**

        1. Pour the batter into the prepared pan and spread it evenly.
        2. If using, sprinkle the streusel topping evenly over the batter.
    5. **Bake the Cake:**
        1. Bake in the preheated oven for 35-45 minutes, or until a toothpick inserted into the center comes out clean and the top is golden brown.
        2. Allow the cake to cool in the pan for 10 minutes before transferring to a wire rack to cool completely.
    6. **Prepare the Glaze (if using):**
        1. In a small bowl, whisk together the powdered sugar and lemon juice or milk until smooth. Adjust the consistency with more liquid or powdered sugar if needed.
    7. **Serve:**
        1. Once the cake has cooled, drizzle the glaze over the top if desired.
        2. Slice and serve the Himbeerkuchen at room temperature. It's delicious on its own or with a dollop of whipped cream.

Himbeerkuchen is a simple yet elegant cake that highlights the fresh, tart flavor of raspberries. Whether you enjoy it with a streusel topping or a sweet glaze, it's a wonderful treat for any occasion!

Hefezopf (Sweet Yeast Bread)

Ingredients:

For the Dough:

- 1 cup (240ml) whole milk
- 1/4 cup (50g) granulated sugar
- 1/4 cup (60g) unsalted butter, softened
- 1 packet (2 1/4 teaspoons) active dry yeast
- 2 large eggs
- 4 cups (500g) all-purpose flour
- 1/2 teaspoon salt
- 1/2 teaspoon ground cinnamon (optional)
- 1/2 teaspoon vanilla extract (optional)
- 1/2 cup (80g) raisins or sultanas (optional)
- 1/4 cup (25g) slivered almonds (optional)

For the Egg Wash:

- 1 large egg
- 1 tablespoon milk

For Garnish (optional):

- Powdered sugar for dusting

Instructions:

1. **Prepare the Yeast Mixture:**
    1. Warm the milk to about 110°F (45°C). Stir in the granulated sugar until dissolved.
    2. Sprinkle the yeast over the milk mixture and let it sit for about 5-10 minutes, until it becomes frothy.
2. **Prepare the Dough:**
    1. In a large bowl, mix the flour, salt, and ground cinnamon (if using).
    2. Make a well in the center and add the yeast mixture, softened butter, and eggs.
    3. Mix until a soft dough forms. If using, fold in the raisins or sultanas.
    4. Turn the dough out onto a floured surface and knead for about 8-10 minutes, or until the dough is smooth and elastic.
3. **Let the Dough Rise:**
    1. Place the dough in a lightly greased bowl, cover with a damp cloth or plastic wrap, and let it rise in a warm place for about 1-1.5 hours, or until doubled in size.
4. **Shape the Hefezopf:**
    1. Punch down the dough and turn it out onto a floured surface. Divide the dough into three equal parts.
    2. Roll each part into a long rope, about 14-16 inches (35-40 cm) long.
    3. Braid the three ropes together and pinch the ends to seal them.
    4. Transfer the braided loaf to a parchment-lined baking sheet.

5. **Let the Bread Rise:**
    1. Cover the braided loaf with a damp cloth and let it rise for another 30-45 minutes, or until puffy.
6. **Prepare the Egg Wash:**
    1. In a small bowl, whisk together the egg and milk. Brush this mixture over the top of the loaf.
7. **Bake the Hefezopf:**
    1. Preheat your oven to 350°F (175°C).
    2. Bake the bread in the preheated oven for 25-30 minutes, or until golden brown and a hollow sound is produced when tapped on the bottom.
8. **Cool and Garnish:**
    1. Allow the Hefezopf to cool on a wire rack.
    2. If desired, dust with powdered sugar before serving.

Hefezopf is perfect for breakfast, brunch, or a special treat with coffee or tea. Its soft texture and slightly sweet flavor make it a favorite in German-speaking countries and beyond. Enjoy!

Erdbeerkuchen (Strawberry Cake)

Ingredients:

For the Sponge Cake:

- 1 cup (200g) granulated sugar
- 1/2 cup (115g) unsalted butter, softened
- 2 large eggs
- 1 teaspoon vanilla extract
- 1 1/2 cups (190g) all-purpose flour
- 1 1/2 teaspoons baking powder
- 1/4 teaspoon salt
- 1/2 cup (120ml) milk

For the Strawberry Topping:

- 1 pound (450g) fresh strawberries, hulled and sliced
- 1/4 cup (50g) granulated sugar (for macerating strawberries)

For the Glaze:

- 1/2 cup (120ml) strawberry juice or water
- 1/4 cup (50g) granulated sugar
- 1 tablespoon cornstarch
- 1 tablespoon lemon juice (optional, for added tanginess)

For Garnish (optional):

- Whipped cream or vanilla ice cream

Instructions:

1. **Prepare the Sponge Cake:**
    1. Preheat your oven to 350°F (175°C). Grease and flour an 8-inch round cake pan or line it with parchment paper.
    2. In a large bowl, cream together the sugar and softened butter until light and fluffy.
    3. Beat in the eggs one at a time, mixing well after each addition. Stir in the vanilla extract.
    4. In a separate bowl, whisk together the flour, baking powder, and salt.
    5. Gradually add the dry ingredients to the butter mixture, alternating with the milk, beginning and ending with the dry ingredients. Mix until just combined.
    6. Pour the batter into the prepared cake pan and smooth the top.
    7. Bake in the preheated oven for 25-30 minutes, or until a toothpick inserted into the center comes out clean. Allow the cake to cool in the pan for 10 minutes before transferring to a wire rack to cool completely.
2. **Prepare the Strawberry Topping:**

1. While the cake is cooling, place the sliced strawberries in a bowl and toss with 1/4 cup of granulated sugar. Let them sit for about 30 minutes to macerate and release their juices.

3. **Prepare the Glaze:**
    1. In a small saucepan, combine the strawberry juice (or water), granulated sugar, and cornstarch. Stir to dissolve the cornstarch.
    2. Cook over medium heat, stirring constantly, until the mixture comes to a boil and thickens. Remove from heat and stir in the lemon juice if using. Let the glaze cool slightly.
4. **Assemble the Cake:**
    1. Once the cake is completely cooled, spread the macerated strawberries evenly over the top of the cake.
    2. Brush or spoon the strawberry glaze over the strawberries to give them a glossy finish.
5. **Serve:**
    1. Garnish with whipped cream or a scoop of vanilla ice cream if desired.
    2. Slice and serve the Erdbeerkuchen. It's best enjoyed the day it's made, but can be stored in the refrigerator for a day or two.

Erdbeerkuchen is a fresh and flavorful dessert that highlights the beauty of strawberries. Whether served at a special occasion or as a simple treat, it's sure to be a crowd-pleaser. Enjoy your strawberry-filled delight!

Kokosnusstorte (Coconut Cake)

Ingredients:

For the Cake:

- 1 1/2 cups (190g) all-purpose flour
- 1 1/2 teaspoons baking powder
- 1/2 teaspoon salt
- 1/2 cup (115g) unsalted butter, softened
- 1 cup (200g) granulated sugar
- 2 large eggs
- 1 cup (240ml) coconut milk (or whole milk)
- 1 teaspoon vanilla extract
- 1 cup (85g) shredded unsweetened coconut

For the Frosting:

- 1 cup (240ml) heavy cream
- 1/4 cup (30g) powdered sugar
- 1 teaspoon vanilla extract
- 1 cup (85g) shredded unsweetened coconut, toasted

For Garnish (optional):

- Additional toasted coconut
- Fresh coconut slices or coconut flakes

Instructions:

1. **Preheat the Oven:**
    1. Preheat your oven to 350°F (175°C). Grease and flour two 8-inch round cake pans or line them with parchment paper.
2. **Prepare the Cake Batter:**
    1. In a medium bowl, whisk together the flour, baking powder, and salt. Set aside.
    2. In a large bowl, cream together the softened butter and granulated sugar until light and fluffy.
    3. Beat in the eggs one at a time, mixing well after each addition. Stir in the vanilla extract.
    4. Gradually add the dry ingredients to the butter mixture, alternating with the coconut milk, beginning and ending with the dry ingredients. Mix until just combined.
    5. Gently fold in the shredded coconut.
3. **Bake the Cake:**
    1. Divide the batter evenly between the prepared cake pans and smooth the tops.
    2. Bake in the preheated oven for 25-30 minutes, or until a toothpick inserted into the center comes out clean and the cakes are golden brown.

3. Allow the cakes to cool in the pans for 10 minutes before transferring to a wire rack to cool completely.
4. **Prepare the Frosting:**
    1. In a large bowl, whip the heavy cream with powdered sugar and vanilla extract until stiff peaks form.
    2. Once the cakes are completely cool, spread a layer of whipped cream frosting on top of one of the cakes. Place the second cake on top.
5. **Frost the Cake:**
    1. Spread the remaining whipped cream frosting evenly over the top and sides of the cake.
    2. Press the toasted shredded coconut onto the sides and top of the cake for a decorative finish.
6. **Garnish (optional):**
    1. Garnish with additional toasted coconut, fresh coconut slices, or coconut flakes if desired.
7. **Serve:**
    1. Slice and serve the Kokosnusstorte. It can be enjoyed immediately or stored in the refrigerator for up to 3 days.

This Coconut Cake combines the soft, fluffy texture of a classic cake with the delightful flavor of coconut, making it a perfect choice for coconut lovers and special occasions. Enjoy your tropical treat!

Tropfen Kuchen (Droplet Cake)

Ingredients:

For the Cake:

- 1 cup (200g) granulated sugar
- 1/2 cup (115g) unsalted butter, softened
- 2 large eggs
- 1 cup (240ml) milk
- 2 cups (250g) all-purpose flour
- 2 teaspoons baking powder
- 1/4 teaspoon salt
- 1 teaspoon vanilla extract

For the Topping:

- 1/4 cup (50g) granulated sugar
- 1/4 cup (60g) unsalted butter, melted
- 1/4 cup (25g) sliced almonds (optional)
- Powdered sugar for dusting (optional)

Instructions:

1. **Preheat the Oven:**
    1. Preheat your oven to 350°F (175°C). Grease and flour a 9-inch round cake pan or a similar-sized baking dish.
2. **Prepare the Cake Batter:**
    1. In a medium bowl, whisk together the flour, baking powder, and salt. Set aside.
    2. In a large bowl, cream together the softened butter and granulated sugar until light and fluffy.
    3. Beat in the eggs one at a time, mixing well after each addition. Stir in the vanilla extract.
    4. Gradually add the dry ingredients to the butter mixture, alternating with the milk, beginning and ending with the dry ingredients. Mix until just combined.
3. **Prepare the Topping:**
    1. In a small bowl, mix the granulated sugar with the melted butter.
    2. If using, stir in the sliced almonds.
4. **Assemble the Cake:**
    1. Pour the batter into the prepared cake pan and smooth the top.
    2. Using the back of a spoon or your fingers, create small dimples or droplets on the surface of the batter. You can make these dimples as deep or shallow as you like.
    3. Spoon or drizzle the sugar-butter mixture evenly over the surface of the batter. If using, sprinkle with sliced almonds.
5. **Bake the Cake:**

1. Bake in the preheated oven for 30-35 minutes, or until a toothpick inserted into the center comes out clean and the top is golden brown.
   2. Allow the cake to cool in the pan for 10 minutes before transferring to a wire rack to cool completely.
6. **Serve:**
   1. Dust the cooled cake with powdered sugar if desired.
   2. Slice and serve. Tropfen Kuchen is delicious on its own or with a cup of coffee or tea.

This Tropfen Kuchen recipe is simple yet flavorful, and its unique appearance makes it a charming addition to any dessert table. Enjoy!

Kirschkuchen (Cherry Cake)

Ingredients:

For the Cake:

- 1 1/2 cups (190g) all-purpose flour
- 1 cup (200g) granulated sugar
- 1/2 cup (115g) unsalted butter, softened
- 2 large eggs
- 1/2 cup (120ml) milk
- 1 1/2 teaspoons baking powder
- 1/4 teaspoon salt
- 1 teaspoon vanilla extract
- 1 cup (150g) fresh or canned cherries, pitted and halved (if using canned, drain and pat dry)

For the Cherry Filling (optional):

- 1 cup (150g) cherries, pitted and chopped
- 1/4 cup (50g) granulated sugar
- 1 tablespoon cornstarch
- 1 tablespoon lemon juice

For the Topping (optional):

- 1/4 cup (50g) granulated sugar
- 1 tablespoon unsalted butter, melted

For Garnish (optional):

- Powdered sugar for dusting

Instructions:

1. **Preheat the Oven:**
    1. Preheat your oven to 350°F (175°C). Grease and flour a 9-inch round cake pan or line it with parchment paper.
2. **Prepare the Cherry Filling (if using):**
    1. In a medium bowl, combine the cherries, granulated sugar, cornstarch, and lemon juice. Toss to coat the cherries evenly and set aside.
3. **Prepare the Cake Batter:**
    1. In a medium bowl, whisk together the flour, baking powder, and salt. Set aside.
    2. In a large bowl, cream together the softened butter and granulated sugar until light and fluffy.

3. Beat in the eggs one at a time, mixing well after each addition. Stir in the vanilla extract.
4. Gradually add the dry ingredients to the butter mixture, alternating with the milk, beginning and ending with the dry ingredients. Mix until just combined.
5. Gently fold in the cherries, being careful not to break them up too much.

4. **Assemble the Cake:**
    1. Pour the batter into the prepared cake pan and spread it evenly.
    2. If using, spoon the cherry filling evenly over the top of the batter.
5. **Prepare the Topping (optional):**
    1. In a small bowl, mix the granulated sugar with the melted butter.
    2. Sprinkle this mixture over the top of the cake batter.
6. **Bake the Cake:**
    1. Bake in the preheated oven for 35-45 minutes, or until a toothpick inserted into the center comes out clean and the top is golden brown.
    2. Allow the cake to cool in the pan for 10 minutes before transferring to a wire rack to cool completely.
7. **Serve:**
    1. Dust with powdered sugar if desired.
    2. Slice and serve. Kirschkuchen is delicious on its own or with a dollop of whipped cream.

This Cherry Cake is a delightful way to enjoy the juicy sweetness of cherries, whether you use fresh or canned ones. It's perfect for a summer treat or a cozy dessert year-round. Enjoy!

Puddingkuchen (Pudding Cake)

Ingredients:

For the Cake Base:

- 1 1/2 cups (190g) all-purpose flour
- 1 cup (200g) granulated sugar
- 1/2 cup (115g) unsalted butter, softened
- 2 large eggs
- 1 teaspoon vanilla extract
- 1 1/2 teaspoons baking powder
- 1/4 teaspoon salt
- 1/2 cup (120ml) milk

For the Pudding Layer:

- 2 cups (480ml) whole milk
- 1/2 cup (100g) granulated sugar
- 1/4 cup (25g) cornstarch
- 1/4 teaspoon salt
- 2 large egg yolks
- 1 teaspoon vanilla extract

For the Topping (optional):

- Powdered sugar for dusting
- Fresh fruit or berries (optional)

Instructions:

1. **Preheat the Oven:**
   1. Preheat your oven to 350°F (175°C). Grease and flour an 8-inch square or round cake pan, or line it with parchment paper.
2. **Prepare the Cake Base:**
   1. In a medium bowl, whisk together the flour, baking powder, and salt. Set aside.
   2. In a large bowl, cream together the softened butter and granulated sugar until light and fluffy.
   3. Beat in the eggs one at a time, mixing well after each addition. Stir in the vanilla extract.
   4. Gradually add the dry ingredients to the butter mixture, alternating with the milk, beginning and ending with the dry ingredients. Mix until just combined.
   5. Pour the batter into the prepared cake pan and smooth the top.
3. **Prepare the Pudding Layer:**
   1. In a medium saucepan, whisk together the milk, sugar, cornstarch, and salt.

2. Cook over medium heat, stirring constantly, until the mixture begins to thicken and comes to a boil. Continue cooking for an additional 1-2 minutes until the pudding is very thick.
3. Remove from heat and whisk in the egg yolks one at a time. Return the pan to the heat and cook for an additional 1-2 minutes, stirring constantly, until the pudding is thick and smooth.
4. Remove from heat and stir in the vanilla extract. Let the pudding cool slightly.

4. **Assemble the Cake:**
   1. Pour the slightly cooled pudding mixture over the batter in the cake pan. Spread the pudding evenly over the cake batter.
5. **Bake the Cake:**
   1. Bake in the preheated oven for 35-45 minutes, or until the cake is set and the top is golden brown. The cake may appear slightly jiggly in the center but will firm up as it cools.
   2. Allow the cake to cool in the pan for 10 minutes before transferring to a wire rack to cool completely.
6. **Serve:**
   1. Dust with powdered sugar if desired.
   2. Garnish with fresh fruit or berries if you like.
   3. Slice and serve. Puddingkuchen can be enjoyed warm or at room temperature.

This Pudding Cake offers a lovely combination of soft, moist cake with a rich, creamy pudding layer. It's a comforting dessert that pairs wonderfully with a cup of coffee or tea. Enjoy!

Schmandkuchen (Sour Cream Cake)

Ingredients:

For the Cake Base:

- 1 1/2 cups (190g) all-purpose flour
- 1 cup (200g) granulated sugar
- 1/2 cup (115g) unsalted butter, softened
- 2 large eggs
- 1 cup (240ml) sour cream
- 1 teaspoon vanilla extract
- 1 1/2 teaspoons baking powder
- 1/4 teaspoon salt

For the Topping:

- 1 cup (240ml) sour cream
- 1/4 cup (50g) granulated sugar
- 1 teaspoon vanilla extract

Optional Add-ins:

- 1 cup (150g) fresh fruit, such as berries or sliced apples (optional)

Instructions:

1. **Preheat the Oven:**
    1. Preheat your oven to 350°F (175°C). Grease and flour a 9-inch round cake pan or line it with parchment paper.
2. **Prepare the Cake Base:**
    1. In a medium bowl, whisk together the flour, baking powder, and salt. Set aside.
    2. In a large bowl, cream together the softened butter and granulated sugar until light and fluffy.
    3. Beat in the eggs one at a time, mixing well after each addition. Stir in the vanilla extract.
    4. Gradually add the dry ingredients to the butter mixture, alternating with the sour cream, beginning and ending with the dry ingredients. Mix until just combined.
    5. If using fresh fruit, gently fold it into the batter.
3. **Bake the Cake:**
    1. Pour the batter into the prepared cake pan and smooth the top.
    2. Bake in the preheated oven for 25-30 minutes, or until a toothpick inserted into the center comes out clean and the cake is golden brown.
    3. Allow the cake to cool in the pan for 10 minutes before transferring to a wire rack to cool completely.
4. **Prepare the Topping:**

1. In a medium bowl, mix together the sour cream, granulated sugar, and vanilla extract until smooth and well combined.
2. Once the cake is completely cooled, spread the sour cream topping evenly over the top.

5. **Serve:**
    1. Slice and serve. Schmandkuchen can be enjoyed on its own or with a cup of coffee or tea.
    2. It's also delicious with a dusting of powdered sugar or a sprinkle of additional fresh fruit on top.

This Sour Cream Cake is a wonderful combination of rich, moist cake with a creamy, tangy topping. It's perfect for any occasion, whether you're hosting a gathering or just looking for a comforting treat. Enjoy!

Rote Grütze Cake

Ingredients:

For the Cake Base:

- 1 1/2 cups (190g) all-purpose flour
- 1 cup (200g) granulated sugar
- 1/2 cup (115g) unsalted butter, softened
- 2 large eggs
- 1/2 cup (120ml) milk
- 1 1/2 teaspoons baking powder
- 1/4 teaspoon salt
- 1 teaspoon vanilla extract

For the Rote Grütze:

- 2 cups (300g) mixed red berries (e.g., raspberries, strawberries, blackberries, red currants)
- 1/2 cup (100g) granulated sugar
- 1 cup (240ml) water
- 1 tablespoon cornstarch
- 1 tablespoon lemon juice

For the Topping (optional):

- Whipped cream or vanilla ice cream
- Fresh berries for garnish

Instructions:

1. **Prepare the Rote Grütze:**
    1. In a medium saucepan, combine the mixed berries, granulated sugar, and water. Bring to a boil over medium heat, stirring occasionally.
    2. In a small bowl, mix the cornstarch with a few tablespoons of cold water to make a slurry. Stir the slurry into the berry mixture.
    3. Continue to cook for 3-5 minutes, or until the mixture thickens and becomes syrupy.
    4. Remove from heat and stir in the lemon juice. Let the Rote Grütze cool to room temperature.
2. **Prepare the Cake Base:**
    1. Preheat your oven to 350°F (175°C). Grease and flour a 9-inch round cake pan or line it with parchment paper.
    2. In a medium bowl, whisk together the flour, baking powder, and salt. Set aside.
    3. In a large bowl, cream together the softened butter and granulated sugar until light and fluffy.

4. Beat in the eggs one at a time, mixing well after each addition. Stir in the vanilla extract.
5. Gradually add the dry ingredients to the butter mixture, alternating with the milk, beginning and ending with the dry ingredients. Mix until just combined.

3. **Assemble the Cake:**
    1. Pour half of the cake batter into the prepared cake pan and smooth the top.
    2. Spoon half of the cooled Rote Grütze over the batter, spreading it gently.
    3. Pour the remaining batter over the Rote Grütze and smooth the top.
    4. Spoon the remaining Rote Grütze on top of the batter. You can gently swirl it into the batter if you like, but don't mix it in completely.

4. **Bake the Cake:**
    1. Bake in the preheated oven for 35-45 minutes, or until a toothpick inserted into the center comes out clean and the cake is golden brown.
    2. Allow the cake to cool in the pan for 10 minutes before transferring to a wire rack to cool completely.

5. **Serve:**
    1. Serve the cake at room temperature or chilled.
    2. Garnish with whipped cream or vanilla ice cream and fresh berries if desired.

Rote Grütze Cake offers a delightful mix of flavors and textures, with the tart and sweet berry compote adding a lovely touch to the moist cake base. It's perfect for a special occasion or as a treat for any time of year. Enjoy!

Butterkuchen (Butter Cake)

Ingredients:

For the Cake Base:

- 1 3/4 cups (220g) all-purpose flour
- 1 cup (200g) granulated sugar
- 1/2 cup (115g) unsalted butter, softened
- 2 large eggs
- 1/2 cup (120ml) milk
- 1 teaspoon vanilla extract
- 2 teaspoons baking powder
- 1/4 teaspoon salt

For the Topping:

- 1/4 cup (50g) granulated sugar
- 1/4 cup (60g) unsalted butter, melted
- 1 teaspoon ground cinnamon (optional)
- 1/2 cup (75g) sliced almonds (optional)

Instructions:

1. **Preheat the Oven:**
    1. Preheat your oven to 350°F (175°C). Grease and flour a 9x13-inch baking pan, or line it with parchment paper.
2. **Prepare the Cake Base:**
    1. In a medium bowl, whisk together the flour, baking powder, and salt. Set aside.
    2. In a large bowl, cream together the softened butter and granulated sugar until light and fluffy.
    3. Beat in the eggs one at a time, mixing well after each addition. Stir in the vanilla extract.
    4. Gradually add the dry ingredients to the butter mixture, alternating with the milk, beginning and ending with the dry ingredients. Mix until just combined.
3. **Assemble the Cake:**
    1. Pour the batter into the prepared baking pan and smooth the top with a spatula.
4. **Prepare the Topping:**
    1. In a small bowl, mix the granulated sugar with the melted butter. If using cinnamon, mix it in as well.
    2. Pour or drizzle this mixture evenly over the top of the cake batter.
    3. If desired, sprinkle the sliced almonds over the top.
5. **Bake the Cake:**
    1. Bake in the preheated oven for 25-30 minutes, or until a toothpick inserted into the center comes out clean and the cake is golden brown.

2. Allow the cake to cool in the pan for 10 minutes before transferring to a wire rack to cool completely.
6. **Serve:**
    1. Slice and serve the Butterkuchen. It's delicious on its own or with a cup of coffee or tea.

Butterkuchen is a simple yet indulgent cake that highlights the rich flavor of butter and the sweetness of sugar. Its light, tender crumb and slightly crisp topping make it a favorite for any occasion. Enjoy!

Bananenkuchen (Banana Cake)

Ingredients:

For the Cake:

- 1 1/2 cups (190g) all-purpose flour
- 1 cup (200g) granulated sugar
- 1/2 cup (115g) unsalted butter, softened
- 2 large eggs
- 1 cup (240ml) mashed ripe bananas (about 2-3 medium bananas)
- 1/4 cup (60ml) milk
- 1 teaspoon vanilla extract
- 1 1/2 teaspoons baking powder
- 1/2 teaspoon baking soda
- 1/4 teaspoon salt
- 1/2 teaspoon ground cinnamon (optional)

For the Optional Cream Cheese Frosting:

- 4 oz (115g) cream cheese, softened
- 1/4 cup (60g) unsalted butter, softened
- 2 cups (240g) powdered sugar
- 1 teaspoon vanilla extract

For Garnish (optional):

- Sliced bananas
- Chopped nuts (e.g., walnuts or pecans)
- Extra powdered sugar for dusting

Instructions:

1. **Preheat the Oven:**
   1. Preheat your oven to 350°F (175°C). Grease and flour a 9-inch round cake pan, or line it with parchment paper.
2. **Prepare the Cake Batter:**
   1. In a medium bowl, whisk together the flour, baking powder, baking soda, salt, and ground cinnamon (if using). Set aside.
   2. In a large bowl, cream together the softened butter and granulated sugar until light and fluffy.
   3. Beat in the eggs one at a time, mixing well after each addition. Stir in the vanilla extract.
   4. Mix in the mashed bananas.
   5. Gradually add the dry ingredients to the butter mixture, alternating with the milk, beginning and ending with the dry ingredients. Mix until just combined.

3. **Bake the Cake:**
   1. Pour the batter into the prepared cake pan and smooth the top.
   2. Bake in the preheated oven for 30-35 minutes, or until a toothpick inserted into the center comes out clean and the cake is golden brown.
   3. Allow the cake to cool in the pan for 10 minutes before transferring to a wire rack to cool completely.
4. **Prepare the Optional Cream Cheese Frosting (if using):**
   1. In a medium bowl, beat the softened cream cheese and butter together until smooth and creamy.
   2. Gradually add the powdered sugar and beat until well combined and fluffy.
   3. Stir in the vanilla extract.
5. **Frost the Cake (optional):**
   1. Once the cake has cooled completely, spread the cream cheese frosting evenly over the top and sides of the cake.
   2. Garnish with sliced bananas and chopped nuts if desired. Dust with additional powdered sugar for a finishing touch.
6. **Serve:**
   1. Slice and serve the Bananenkuchen. It's delicious on its own or with a cup of coffee or tea.

This Banana Cake is a perfect way to enjoy the natural sweetness of bananas, and the optional cream cheese frosting adds a rich, tangy complement. Enjoy your delightful treat!

Zupfkuchen (Twist Cake)

Ingredients:

For the Dough:

- 1 1/2 cups (190g) all-purpose flour
- 1/2 cup (100g) granulated sugar
- 1/2 cup (115g) unsalted butter, softened
- 1 large egg
- 1 teaspoon baking powder
- 1/4 teaspoon salt

For the Cheesecake Filling:

- 2 cups (450g) cream cheese, softened
- 1 cup (200g) granulated sugar
- 2 large eggs
- 1 teaspoon vanilla extract
- 1 cup (240ml) sour cream
- 1 tablespoon all-purpose flour

For the Topping (optional):

- Powdered sugar for dusting

Instructions:

1. **Prepare the Dough:**
   1. In a medium bowl, whisk together the flour, baking powder, and salt. Set aside.
   2. In a large bowl, cream together the softened butter and granulated sugar until light and fluffy.
   3. Beat in the egg until well combined.
   4. Gradually add the dry ingredients to the butter mixture, mixing until a dough forms. The dough will be soft and slightly sticky.
2. **Prepare the Cheesecake Filling:**
   1. In a large bowl, beat the cream cheese until smooth.
   2. Add the granulated sugar and beat until well combined.
   3. Beat in the eggs one at a time, mixing well after each addition.
   4. Stir in the vanilla extract, sour cream, and flour until smooth and well combined.
3. **Assemble the Cake:**
   1. Preheat your oven to 350°F (175°C). Grease and flour a 9-inch round springform pan or line it with parchment paper.
   2. Divide the dough in half. Press one half of the dough evenly into the bottom of the prepared pan to form the base layer.
   3. Pour the cheesecake filling over the dough base and spread it evenly.

4. Pinch or tear the remaining dough into small pieces and scatter them evenly over the top of the cheesecake filling, creating a twisty or crumpled appearance.
4. **Bake the Cake:**
   1. Bake in the preheated oven for 45-50 minutes, or until the filling is set and the top is golden brown.
   2. Allow the cake to cool in the pan for 10 minutes before removing the sides of the springform pan. Cool completely on a wire rack.
5. **Serve:**
   1. Dust with powdered sugar if desired before serving.
   2. Slice and enjoy! Zupfkuchen is great on its own or with a cup of coffee or tea.

Zupfkuchen offers a wonderful combination of creamy cheesecake and buttery dough, making it a favorite treat for gatherings and special occasions. Enjoy this classic German dessert!

Pflaumenkuchen (Plum Cake)

Ingredients:

For the Cake Base:

- 1 3/4 cups (220g) all-purpose flour
- 1 cup (200g) granulated sugar
- 1/2 cup (115g) unsalted butter, softened
- 2 large eggs
- 1/2 cup (120ml) milk
- 1 teaspoon vanilla extract
- 2 teaspoons baking powder
- 1/4 teaspoon salt

For the Plum Topping:

- 4-5 medium plums, pitted and sliced
- 1/4 cup (50g) granulated sugar
- 1 teaspoon ground cinnamon (optional)
- 1 tablespoon lemon juice

For the Optional Streusel Topping:

- 1/2 cup (65g) all-purpose flour
- 1/4 cup (50g) granulated sugar
- 1/4 cup (60g) unsalted butter, cold and cubed

Instructions:

1. **Preheat the Oven:**
    1. Preheat your oven to 350°F (175°C). Grease and flour a 9-inch round or square baking pan, or line it with parchment paper.
2. **Prepare the Cake Base:**
    1. In a medium bowl, whisk together the flour, baking powder, and salt. Set aside.
    2. In a large bowl, cream together the softened butter and granulated sugar until light and fluffy.
    3. Beat in the eggs one at a time, mixing well after each addition. Stir in the vanilla extract.
    4. Gradually add the dry ingredients to the butter mixture, alternating with the milk, beginning and ending with the dry ingredients. Mix until just combined.
    5. Pour the batter into the prepared baking pan and smooth the top.
3. **Prepare the Plum Topping:**
    1. In a medium bowl, toss the plum slices with granulated sugar, ground cinnamon (if using), and lemon juice until evenly coated.
    2. Arrange the plum slices in a single layer over the top of the batter.

4. **Prepare the Streusel Topping (optional):**
    1. In a small bowl, mix the flour and granulated sugar.
    2. Cut in the cold, cubed butter using a pastry cutter or your fingers until the mixture resembles coarse crumbs.
    3. Sprinkle the streusel evenly over the plums.
5. **Bake the Cake:**
    1. Bake in the preheated oven for 35-45 minutes, or until the cake is golden brown and a toothpick inserted into the center comes out clean.
    2. Allow the cake to cool in the pan for 10 minutes before transferring to a wire rack to cool completely.
6. **Serve:**
    1. Slice and serve the Pflaumenkuchen at room temperature.
    2. It's delicious on its own or with a dollop of whipped cream or a scoop of vanilla ice cream.

This Plum Cake combines a soft, buttery cake with the vibrant flavor of fresh plums, making it a delightful dessert for any occasion. Enjoy this classic treat!

Marillenknödel (Apricot Dumplings)

Ingredients:

For the Dough:

- 1 cup (250g) quark or ricotta cheese (you can also use farmer's cheese or a mix of cream cheese and yogurt)
- 1 large egg
- 1/4 cup (50g) granulated sugar
- 1 1/2 cups (190g) all-purpose flour
- 1/2 cup (60g) semolina or cornstarch
- 1/4 teaspoon salt
- 1 teaspoon vanilla extract

For the Filling:

- 8-10 apricots, pitted (fresh or well-drained canned apricots)
- 2 tablespoons granulated sugar (for sprinkling on apricots)
- 1 teaspoon ground cinnamon (optional)

For the Coating:

- 1/4 cup (50g) unsalted butter
- 1/2 cup (60g) breadcrumbs
- 1/4 cup (50g) granulated sugar
- 1 teaspoon ground cinnamon

Instructions:

1. **Prepare the Apricots:**
    1. If using fresh apricots, wash them, cut them in half, and remove the pits.
    2. Sprinkle the apricot halves with granulated sugar and ground cinnamon (if using). Set aside.
2. **Prepare the Dough:**
    1. In a large bowl, mix together the quark (or ricotta cheese), egg, and granulated sugar until smooth.
    2. Gradually add the flour, semolina (or cornstarch), and salt, mixing until a soft dough forms. The dough should be slightly sticky but manageable. If it's too sticky, add a little more flour.
3. **Form the Dumplings:**
    1. On a lightly floured surface, divide the dough into 8-10 equal portions.
    2. Flatten each portion into a small circle about 3-4 inches in diameter.
    3. Place one apricot in the center of each dough circle.
    4. Carefully fold the dough around the apricot, pinching the edges together to seal completely. Roll the dumpling gently between your hands to form a smooth ball.

Eierlikörtorte (Egg Liqueur Cake)

Ingredients:

For the Cake:

- 1 1/2 cups (190g) all-purpose flour
- 1 cup (200g) granulated sugar
- 1/2 cup (115g) unsalted butter, softened
- 3 large eggs
- 1/2 cup (120ml) milk
- 1/2 cup (120ml) Eierlikör (egg liqueur)
- 1 teaspoon vanilla extract
- 1 1/2 teaspoons baking powder
- 1/4 teaspoon salt

For the Filling:

- 1 cup (240ml) heavy cream
- 2 tablespoons granulated sugar
- 1/2 cup (120ml) Eierlikör

For the Frosting:

- 1 cup (240ml) heavy cream
- 2 tablespoons powdered sugar
- 1/2 cup (120ml) Eierlikör
- 1 tablespoon unflavored gelatin (optional, to stabilize the cream)

For Garnish (optional):

- Chocolate shavings
- Fresh berries
- Mint leaves

Instructions:

1. **Preheat the Oven:**
    1. Preheat your oven to 350°F (175°C). Grease and flour a 9-inch round springform pan or line it with parchment paper.
2. **Prepare the Cake:**
    1. In a medium bowl, whisk together the flour, baking powder, and salt. Set aside.
    2. In a large bowl, cream together the softened butter and granulated sugar until light and fluffy.
    3. Beat in the eggs one at a time, mixing well after each addition. Stir in the vanilla extract.

1. Bake in the preheated oven for 40-50 minutes, or until a toothpick inserted into the center comes out clean and the cake is golden brown.
2. Allow the cake to cool in the pan for 10 minutes before transferring to a wire rack to cool completely.

6. **Serve:**
    1. Once cooled, you can dust the cake with powdered sugar or drizzle with a simple glaze if desired.

Marble Cake is a delightful treat with a striking appearance and a delicious combination of vanilla and chocolate flavors. It's perfect for any occasion, and its moist, tender crumb makes it a favorite among cake lovers. Enjoy!

Marmorkuchen (Marble Cake)

Ingredients:

For the Cake:

- 1 3/4 cups (220g) all-purpose flour
- 1 1/2 teaspoons baking powder
- 1/4 teaspoon salt
- 1/2 cup (115g) unsalted butter, softened
- 1 cup (200g) granulated sugar
- 3 large eggs
- 1/2 cup (120ml) milk
- 1 teaspoon vanilla extract

For the Chocolate Batter:

- 1/4 cup (25g) unsweetened cocoa powder
- 2 tablespoons granulated sugar
- 2 tablespoons milk

Instructions:

1. **Preheat the Oven:**
    1. Preheat your oven to 350°F (175°C). Grease and flour a 9-inch round or 10-inch Bundt pan, or line it with parchment paper.
2. **Prepare the Vanilla Batter:**
    1. In a medium bowl, whisk together the flour, baking powder, and salt. Set aside.
    2. In a large bowl, cream together the softened butter and granulated sugar until light and fluffy.
    3. Beat in the eggs one at a time, mixing well after each addition. Stir in the vanilla extract.
    4. Gradually add the dry ingredients to the butter mixture, alternating with the milk, beginning and ending with the dry ingredients. Mix until just combined.
3. **Prepare the Chocolate Batter:**
    1. In a small bowl, whisk together the cocoa powder, granulated sugar, and milk until smooth.
4. **Assemble the Marble Cake:**
    1. Divide the vanilla batter in half. Mix one half with the chocolate mixture until well combined.
    2. Spoon alternating dollops of vanilla and chocolate batters into the prepared pan.
    3. Use a knife or skewer to swirl the batters together, creating a marbled effect. Be careful not to overmix, as you want to maintain the marble pattern.
5. **Bake the Cake:**

4. **Cook the Dumplings:**
    1. Bring a large pot of salted water to a boil.
    2. Gently drop the dumplings into the boiling water. Cook for 10-12 minutes, or until the dumplings float to the surface and are cooked through.
    3. Remove the dumplings with a slotted spoon and drain them well.
5. **Prepare the Coating:**
    1. In a medium skillet, melt the butter over medium heat.
    2. Add the breadcrumbs and cook, stirring frequently, until they are golden brown.
    3. In a separate bowl, mix together the granulated sugar and ground cinnamon.
6. **Coat the Dumplings:**
    1. Roll each dumpling in the cinnamon sugar mixture, then gently coat with the toasted breadcrumbs.
7. **Serve:**
    1. Serve the Marillenknödel warm, drizzled with a little melted butter if desired.
    2. You can also sprinkle additional cinnamon sugar on top before serving.

These Apricot Dumplings are a delightful dessert with a perfect combination of sweet apricots and rich, buttery coating. They're wonderful on their own or with a dollop of whipped cream. Enjoy!

4. Gradually add the dry ingredients to the butter mixture, alternating with the milk and Eierlikör, beginning and ending with the dry ingredients. Mix until just combined.
5. Pour the batter into the prepared pan and smooth the top.
6. Bake in the preheated oven for 25-30 minutes, or until a toothpick inserted into the center comes out clean. Allow the cake to cool in the pan for 10 minutes before transferring to a wire rack to cool completely.

3. **Prepare the Filling:**
   1. In a medium bowl, whip the heavy cream with granulated sugar until soft peaks form.
   2. Gently fold in the Eierlikör until well combined. Refrigerate until ready to use.
4. **Prepare the Frosting:**
   1. If using gelatin to stabilize the cream, dissolve the gelatin in a small amount of hot water according to package instructions. Let it cool slightly.
   2. In a medium bowl, whip the heavy cream with powdered sugar until soft peaks form.
   3. Gently fold in the Eierlikör and the dissolved gelatin (if using). Refrigerate until ready to use.
5. **Assemble the Cake:**
   1. If the cake has domed on top, level it with a knife.
   2. Slice the cake horizontally into two layers.
   3. Spread a layer of the Eierlikör filling on the bottom layer of the cake. Place the top layer of the cake over the filling.
   4. Frost the cake with the Eierlikör frosting, smoothing it over the top and sides.
6. **Garnish and Serve:**
   1. Garnish the cake with chocolate shavings, fresh berries, and mint leaves if desired.
   2. Chill the cake in the refrigerator for at least an hour before serving to allow the flavors to meld and the frosting to set.

Eierlikörtorte is a luxurious and flavorful cake that celebrates the rich taste of egg liqueur. It's perfect for special occasions and holiday celebrations. Enjoy!

Quarktorte (Quark Cake)

Ingredients:

For the Crust:

- 1 1/2 cups (150g) graham cracker crumbs or digestive biscuit crumbs
- 1/4 cup (50g) granulated sugar
- 1/2 cup (115g) unsalted butter, melted

For the Filling:

- 2 cups (500g) quark cheese (or use a combination of cream cheese and Greek yogurt as a substitute)
- 1 cup (200g) granulated sugar
- 3 large eggs
- 1 cup (240ml) sour cream or Greek yogurt
- 1 teaspoon vanilla extract
- 1/4 cup (60ml) milk
- 2 tablespoons all-purpose flour or cornstarch
- Zest of 1 lemon (optional)
- Juice of 1 lemon (optional)

For the Topping (optional):

- Fresh fruit (such as berries or sliced fruit)
- Powdered sugar for dusting

Instructions:

1. **Preheat the Oven:**
    1. Preheat your oven to 350°F (175°C). Grease the sides of a 9-inch springform pan or line the bottom with parchment paper.
2. **Prepare the Crust:**
    1. In a medium bowl, combine the graham cracker crumbs (or digestive biscuit crumbs), granulated sugar, and melted butter. Mix until the crumbs are well coated and the mixture resembles wet sand.
    2. Press the crumb mixture into the bottom of the prepared springform pan to form an even crust. Use the back of a spoon to press it down firmly.
    3. Bake the crust in the preheated oven for 10 minutes. Remove from the oven and let it cool while you prepare the filling.
3. **Prepare the Filling:**
    1. In a large bowl, beat the quark cheese with the granulated sugar until smooth and creamy.
    2. Add the eggs one at a time, beating well after each addition.
    3. Mix in the sour cream (or Greek yogurt), vanilla extract, and lemon zest (if using).

4. Gradually add the milk and flour (or cornstarch) to the mixture, beating until smooth and well combined. If using lemon juice, add it at this stage.
   5. Pour the filling over the cooled crust in the springform pan and smooth the top with a spatula.
4. **Bake the Cake:**
   1. Bake in the preheated oven for 50-60 minutes, or until the center is set and the top is lightly golden. The cake should be firm but slightly jiggly in the center.
   2. Turn off the oven and crack the oven door slightly. Let the cake cool in the oven for about an hour. This helps prevent cracking.
   3. Remove the cake from the oven and let it cool completely at room temperature. Refrigerate for at least 4 hours or overnight for the best texture and flavor.
5. **Serve:**
   1. Before serving, you can garnish the cake with fresh fruit and a dusting of powdered sugar if desired.
   2. Run a knife around the edge of the cake to loosen it from the sides of the springform pan, then remove the sides of the pan.

Quarktorte is a creamy and satisfying dessert with a lovely tangy flavor from the quark cheese. It's perfect for any occasion and pairs wonderfully with fresh fruit. Enjoy!

Pfeffernüsse (Pepper Nuts)

Ingredients:

For the Cookies:

- 1/2 cup (115g) unsalted butter, softened
- 1 cup (200g) granulated sugar
- 1/4 cup (60ml) honey or molasses
- 1 large egg
- 2 1/2 cups (315g) all-purpose flour
- 1 teaspoon baking soda
- 1 teaspoon ground cinnamon
- 1/2 teaspoon ground cloves
- 1/2 teaspoon ground ginger
- 1/4 teaspoon ground black pepper
- 1/4 teaspoon ground nutmeg
- 1/4 teaspoon salt
- 1/2 cup (50g) finely chopped nuts (such as walnuts or almonds, optional)

For the Glaze (optional):

- 1 cup (120g) powdered sugar
- 2-3 tablespoons milk or water
- 1/2 teaspoon vanilla extract

Instructions:

1. **Prepare the Dough:**
    1. In a large bowl, cream together the softened butter and granulated sugar until light and fluffy.
    2. Beat in the honey (or molasses) and egg until well combined.
    3. In a separate bowl, whisk together the flour, baking soda, ground cinnamon, ground cloves, ground ginger, ground black pepper, ground nutmeg, and salt.
    4. Gradually add the dry ingredients to the butter mixture, mixing until just combined. If using, fold in the finely chopped nuts.
2. **Shape the Cookies:**
    1. Preheat your oven to 350°F (175°C). Line a baking sheet with parchment paper or a silicone baking mat.
    2. Roll the dough into small balls, about 1 inch (2.5 cm) in diameter, and place them on the prepared baking sheet. Space them about 1 inch apart.
    3. Flatten each ball slightly with the bottom of a glass or your fingers.
3. **Bake the Cookies:**
    1. Bake in the preheated oven for 10-12 minutes, or until the edges are golden brown.

      2. Allow the cookies to cool on the baking sheet for a few minutes before transferring them to a wire rack to cool completely.
4. **Prepare the Glaze (optional):**
      1. In a small bowl, whisk together the powdered sugar, milk (or water), and vanilla extract until smooth.
      2. Dip the cooled cookies into the glaze or drizzle it over the cookies.
      3. Allow the glaze to set before storing the cookies.
5. **Serve and Store:**
      1. Enjoy the Pfeffernüsse as a festive treat with a cup of tea or coffee.
      2. Store the cookies in an airtight container at room temperature for up to 2 weeks.

Pfeffernüsse cookies are a holiday classic with their rich, spiced flavor and satisfying crunch. They make a great addition to any holiday cookie platter or as a delightful treat to enjoy with friends and family. Enjoy!

Zitronenstreuselkuchen (Lemon Crumb Cake)

Ingredients:

For the Cake:

- 1 1/2 cups (190g) all-purpose flour
- 1/2 cup (100g) granulated sugar
- 1/2 cup (115g) unsalted butter, softened
- 1/2 cup (120ml) milk
- 2 large eggs
- 1 teaspoon vanilla extract
- 2 teaspoons baking powder
- 1/4 teaspoon salt
- Zest of 1 lemon
- Juice of 1 lemon (about 2 tablespoons)

For the Crumb Topping:

- 1/2 cup (65g) all-purpose flour
- 1/4 cup (50g) granulated sugar
- 1/4 cup (60g) unsalted butter, cold and cubed
- 1/2 teaspoon ground cinnamon (optional)

For the Lemon Glaze (optional):

- 1 cup (120g) powdered sugar
- 2-3 tablespoons lemon juice

Instructions:

1. **Preheat the Oven:**
    1. Preheat your oven to 350°F (175°C). Grease and flour a 9-inch round or square baking pan, or line it with parchment paper.
2. **Prepare the Cake Batter:**
    1. In a medium bowl, whisk together the flour, baking powder, and salt. Set aside.
    2. In a large bowl, cream together the softened butter and granulated sugar until light and fluffy.
    3. Beat in the eggs one at a time, mixing well after each addition. Stir in the vanilla extract.
    4. Gradually add the dry ingredients to the butter mixture, alternating with the milk, beginning and ending with the dry ingredients. Mix until just combined.
    5. Stir in the lemon zest and lemon juice until evenly distributed.
3. **Prepare the Crumb Topping:**
    1. In a medium bowl, combine the flour, granulated sugar, and ground cinnamon (if using).

2. Cut in the cold, cubed butter using a pastry cutter or your fingers until the mixture resembles coarse crumbs.
4. **Assemble the Cake:**
    1. Pour the cake batter into the prepared pan and smooth the top with a spatula.
    2. Sprinkle the crumb topping evenly over the cake batter.
5. **Bake the Cake:**
    1. Bake in the preheated oven for 35-45 minutes, or until a toothpick inserted into the center comes out clean and the top is golden brown.
    2. Allow the cake to cool in the pan for 10 minutes before transferring to a wire rack to cool completely.
6. **Prepare the Lemon Glaze (optional):**
    1. In a small bowl, whisk together the powdered sugar and lemon juice until smooth. If the glaze is too thick, add a little more lemon juice. If it's too thin, add more powdered sugar.
7. **Glaze and Serve:**
    1. Once the cake is completely cooled, drizzle the lemon glaze over the top.
    2. Let the glaze set before slicing and serving.

This Lemon Crumb Cake is a delicious blend of tangy lemon and buttery crumbs, making it a perfect treat for any occasion. Enjoy it with a cup of tea or coffee for a delightful snack or dessert!

Kirschenmichel (Cherry Michel)

Ingredients:

For the Cherry Mixture:

- 2 cups (500g) pitted cherries (fresh or frozen)
- 1/4 cup (50g) granulated sugar
- 1 tablespoon lemon juice
- 1 teaspoon vanilla extract
- 1 tablespoon cornstarch (optional, to thicken)

For the Bread Mixture:

- 6 cups (about 200g) stale bread or brioche, cubed (crusts removed if desired)
- 2 cups (480ml) milk
- 1/2 cup (100g) granulated sugar
- 3 large eggs
- 1 teaspoon vanilla extract
- 1/2 teaspoon ground cinnamon (optional)
- 1/4 teaspoon salt
- 2 tablespoons unsalted butter, melted (for greasing)

For the Topping (optional):

- Powdered sugar, for dusting
- Whipped cream or vanilla ice cream, for serving

Instructions:

1. **Prepare the Cherry Mixture:**
    1. In a medium saucepan, combine the cherries, granulated sugar, lemon juice, and vanilla extract.
    2. Cook over medium heat until the cherries release their juices and the mixture starts to bubble. If you prefer a thicker filling, dissolve the cornstarch in a small amount of water and stir it into the cherry mixture. Cook for an additional minute until thickened.
    3. Remove from heat and let it cool slightly.
2. **Prepare the Bread Mixture:**
    1. Preheat your oven to 350°F (175°C). Grease a 9-inch square or similar-sized baking dish with melted butter.
    2. In a large bowl, whisk together the milk, granulated sugar, eggs, vanilla extract, ground cinnamon (if using), and salt.
    3. Add the bread cubes to the milk mixture and let them soak for about 10-15 minutes, stirring occasionally, until the bread is well absorbed.
3. **Assemble the Dessert:**

    1. Gently fold the cherry mixture into the soaked bread mixture.
    2. Pour the mixture into the prepared baking dish and spread it out evenly.
4. **Bake the Kirschenmichel:**
    1. Bake in the preheated oven for 40-50 minutes, or until the top is golden brown and the center is set. A toothpick inserted into the center should come out clean.
    2. Allow the Kirschenmichel to cool slightly before serving.
5. **Serve:**
    1. Dust with powdered sugar if desired.
    2. Serve warm, optionally with a dollop of whipped cream or a scoop of vanilla ice cream.

Kirschenmichel is a comforting and delicious way to enjoy cherries, and it's especially great for utilizing leftover bread. Its sweet and fruity flavor, combined with the creamy texture of the bread pudding, makes it a perfect dessert for any season. Enjoy!

Joghurtkuchen mit Beeren (Yogurt Cake with Berries)

Ingredients:

For the Cake:

- 1 cup (240ml) plain yogurt (Greek yogurt works well too)
- 1 cup (200g) granulated sugar
- 1/2 cup (115g) unsalted butter, softened
- 3 large eggs
- 1 teaspoon vanilla extract
- 1 1/2 cups (190g) all-purpose flour
- 2 teaspoons baking powder
- 1/4 teaspoon salt
- 1 cup (150g) fresh or frozen berries (such as blueberries, raspberries, or diced strawberries)

For the Topping (optional):

- Powdered sugar, for dusting
- Additional fresh berries for garnish

Instructions:

1. **Preheat the Oven:**
    1. Preheat your oven to 350°F (175°C). Grease and flour a 9-inch round or square baking pan, or line it with parchment paper.
2. **Prepare the Cake Batter:**
    1. In a large bowl, cream together the softened butter and granulated sugar until light and fluffy.
    2. Beat in the eggs one at a time, mixing well after each addition. Stir in the vanilla extract.
    3. Add the yogurt and mix until smooth.
    4. In a separate bowl, whisk together the flour, baking powder, and salt.
    5. Gradually add the dry ingredients to the wet ingredients, mixing until just combined.
    6. Gently fold in the berries, being careful not to overmix.
3. **Bake the Cake:**
    1. Pour the batter into the prepared baking pan and smooth the top with a spatula.
    2. Bake in the preheated oven for 35-45 minutes, or until a toothpick inserted into the center comes out clean and the top is lightly golden brown.
    3. Allow the cake to cool in the pan for 10 minutes before transferring to a wire rack to cool completely.
4. **Serve:**
    1. Once cooled, you can dust the cake with powdered sugar if desired.

2. Garnish with additional fresh berries for a lovely presentation.

This Yogurt Cake with Berries is a deliciously moist and flavorful treat, perfect for enjoying with a cup of tea or coffee. The yogurt adds a subtle tanginess and keeps the cake tender, while the berries provide bursts of fruity sweetness. Enjoy!

Zebrakuchen (Zebra Cake)

Ingredients:

For the Cake Batter:

- 1 1/2 cups (190g) all-purpose flour
- 1 1/2 teaspoons baking powder
- 1/4 teaspoon salt
- 1/2 cup (115g) unsalted butter, softened
- 1 cup (200g) granulated sugar
- 3 large eggs
- 1/2 cup (120ml) milk
- 1 teaspoon vanilla extract
- 1/2 cup (50g) unsweetened cocoa powder
- 2 tablespoons boiling water (for cocoa powder)

Instructions:

1. **Preheat the Oven:**
    1. Preheat your oven to 350°F (175°C). Grease and flour a 9-inch round or 10-inch Bundt pan, or line it with parchment paper.
2. **Prepare the Vanilla Batter:**
    1. In a medium bowl, whisk together the flour, baking powder, and salt. Set aside.
    2. In a large bowl, cream together the softened butter and granulated sugar until light and fluffy.
    3. Beat in the eggs one at a time, mixing well after each addition. Stir in the vanilla extract.
    4. Gradually add the dry ingredients to the butter mixture, alternating with the milk, beginning and ending with the dry ingredients. Mix until just combined.
3. **Prepare the Chocolate Batter:**
    1. In a small bowl, mix the cocoa powder with the boiling water until smooth and well combined.
    2. Gently fold the cocoa mixture into half of the vanilla batter, creating the chocolate batter.
4. **Assemble the Cake:**
    1. Start by pouring a few tablespoons of the vanilla batter into the center of the prepared pan.
    2. Spoon a few tablespoons of the chocolate batter on top of the vanilla batter, in the center. Continue to alternate between the vanilla and chocolate batters, pouring each new layer in the center of the previous one. This will create concentric circles of batter.
    3. Do not spread or smooth the batter; let the batter naturally spread and create the zebra effect.
5. **Bake the Cake:**

1. Bake in the preheated oven for 40-50 minutes, or until a toothpick inserted into the center comes out clean and the top is golden brown.
   2. Allow the cake to cool in the pan for 10 minutes before transferring to a wire rack to cool completely.
6. **Serve:**
   1. Once cooled, you can dust the cake with powdered sugar or drizzle with a simple glaze or chocolate ganache if desired.

Tips for Success:

- **Consistency:** Ensure that the batters are of similar consistency to create clear stripes. If one is too thick or thin, it might not create the desired effect.
- **Pouring Technique:** Pour the batters into the center of the pan without spreading them to maintain the striped pattern.
- **Cooling:** Allow the cake to cool completely before slicing to get the best visual effect of the zebra stripes.

Zebrakuchen is a delightful and impressive cake that combines the flavors of vanilla and chocolate with a visually appealing pattern. It's perfect for any celebration or as a fun baking project. Enjoy!

Kirschtorte (Cherry Torte)

Ingredients:

For the Sponge Cake:

- 4 large eggs
- 1 cup (200g) granulated sugar
- 1 cup (125g) all-purpose flour
- 1 teaspoon baking powder
- 1/4 teaspoon salt
- 1/4 cup (60ml) milk
- 1/4 cup (60ml) vegetable oil
- 1 teaspoon vanilla extract

For the Cherry Filling:

- 2 cups (500g) pitted cherries (fresh or frozen)
- 1/2 cup (100g) granulated sugar
- 1 tablespoon lemon juice
- 1 tablespoon cornstarch (optional, to thicken)
- 1/2 cup (120ml) cherry juice or water

For the Cream Filling and Topping:

- 1 1/2 cups (360ml) heavy cream
- 2 tablespoons powdered sugar
- 1 teaspoon vanilla extract

For the Decoration (optional):

- Additional cherries for topping
- Chocolate shavings or grated chocolate

Instructions:

1. **Prepare the Sponge Cake:**
    1. Preheat your oven to 350°F (175°C). Grease and flour two 8-inch round cake pans or line them with parchment paper.
    2. In a large bowl, beat the eggs and granulated sugar with an electric mixer until pale and fluffy.
    3. In a separate bowl, sift together the flour, baking powder, and salt.
    4. Gently fold the dry ingredients into the egg mixture.
    5. In a small bowl, combine the milk, vegetable oil, and vanilla extract. Fold this mixture into the batter until just combined.

6. Divide the batter evenly between the prepared pans and smooth the tops with a spatula.
7. Bake in the preheated oven for 20-25 minutes, or until a toothpick inserted into the center comes out clean.
8. Let the cakes cool in the pans for 10 minutes before transferring to a wire rack to cool completely.

2. **Prepare the Cherry Filling:**
    1. In a medium saucepan, combine the cherries, granulated sugar, lemon juice, and cherry juice (or water).
    2. Cook over medium heat until the cherries release their juices and the mixture starts to bubble.
    3. If you prefer a thicker filling, dissolve the cornstarch in a small amount of cold water and stir it into the cherry mixture. Cook for an additional minute until thickened.
    4. Remove from heat and let it cool to room temperature.
3. **Prepare the Cream Filling and Topping:**
    1. In a large bowl, beat the heavy cream with an electric mixer until it begins to thicken.
    2. Add the powdered sugar and vanilla extract, and continue to beat until stiff peaks form.
4. **Assemble the Torte:**
    1. Once the cakes are completely cooled, slice each cake in half horizontally to create four layers.
    2. Place one layer of cake on a serving plate or cake stand. Spread a layer of cherry filling over the cake.
    3. Add a layer of whipped cream over the cherries.
    4. Repeat with the remaining layers, ending with a layer of cake on top.
    5. Frost the top and sides of the torte with the remaining whipped cream.
5. **Decorate:**
    1. Decorate the top of the torte with additional cherries and chocolate shavings or grated chocolate, if desired.
6. **Serve:**
    1. Chill the torte in the refrigerator for at least an hour to allow the flavors to meld and the cake to set.
    2. Slice and serve chilled.

Kirschtorte is a rich and satisfying cake with a perfect balance of sweet and tart flavors. It's an elegant choice for any celebration and is sure to impress your guests with its delicious layers and beautiful presentation. Enjoy!

Wiener Apfelstrudel (Viennese Apple Strudel)

Ingredients:

For the Dough:

- 2 cups (250g) all-purpose flour
- 1/2 teaspoon salt
- 1 large egg
- 1/2 cup (120ml) warm water
- 2 tablespoons vegetable oil or melted butter

For the Apple Filling:

- 6 medium apples (such as Granny Smith or Jonagold), peeled, cored, and thinly sliced
- 1/2 cup (100g) granulated sugar
- 1 teaspoon ground cinnamon
- 1/4 teaspoon ground nutmeg
- 1/4 teaspoon ground cloves (optional)
- 1 tablespoon lemon juice
- 1/4 cup (30g) raisins
- 1/4 cup (30g) chopped walnuts or almonds (optional)
- 1/2 cup (60g) fresh breadcrumbs (to absorb moisture)

For Assembly:

- 3 tablespoons melted butter (for brushing the dough)
- Powdered sugar, for dusting

Instructions:

1. **Prepare the Dough:**
    1. In a large bowl, mix the flour and salt.
    2. In a small bowl, whisk together the egg, warm water, and vegetable oil.
    3. Gradually add the wet ingredients to the flour mixture, mixing until a dough forms.
    4. Knead the dough on a lightly floured surface for about 5-7 minutes until smooth and elastic.
    5. Place the dough in a lightly oiled bowl, cover it with plastic wrap or a damp cloth, and let it rest for at least 30 minutes at room temperature.
2. **Prepare the Apple Filling:**
    1. In a large bowl, combine the sliced apples, granulated sugar, cinnamon, nutmeg, cloves (if using), lemon juice, raisins, and chopped nuts (if using).
    2. Toss everything together until the apples are evenly coated.
3. **Roll Out the Dough:**
    1. Preheat your oven to 375°F (190°C). Line a baking sheet with parchment paper.

2. On a lightly floured surface, roll out the dough into a large, thin rectangle (about 16x24 inches or 40x60 cm).
   3. Gently stretch the dough with your hands if necessary to achieve a thin layer. The dough should be thin enough to see through.
4. **Assemble the Strudel:**
   1. Brush the entire surface of the dough with melted butter.
   2. Sprinkle the fresh breadcrumbs evenly over the dough, leaving a 1-inch (2.5 cm) border around the edges. The breadcrumbs help absorb moisture from the filling.
   3. Evenly spread the apple mixture over the breadcrumbs.
   4. Carefully lift one edge of the dough and start rolling it up tightly, like a jelly roll or log. Use the parchment paper to help with the rolling process and ensure the strudel stays tight.
   5. Place the rolled strudel seam-side down on the prepared baking sheet.
   6. Brush the top of the strudel with more melted butter.
5. **Bake the Strudel:**
   1. Bake in the preheated oven for 35-45 minutes, or until the strudel is golden brown and crispy.
   2. If necessary, rotate the baking sheet halfway through baking to ensure even browning.
6. **Serve:**
   1. Allow the strudel to cool slightly before slicing.
   2. Dust with powdered sugar just before serving.
   3. Serve warm, with a dollop of whipped cream or a scoop of vanilla ice cream if desired.

Wiener Apfelstrudel is a timeless dessert with a deliciously flaky crust and a sweet, spiced apple filling. Its distinctive layers and comforting flavors make it a perfect treat for any occasion. Enjoy this delightful Viennese classic!

Birnen-Schokoladenkuchen (Pear Chocolate Cake)

Ingredients:

For the Cake:

- 1 cup (125g) all-purpose flour
- 1/2 cup (50g) unsweetened cocoa powder
- 1 teaspoon baking powder
- 1/2 teaspoon baking soda
- 1/4 teaspoon salt
- 1/2 cup (115g) unsalted butter, softened
- 1 cup (200g) granulated sugar
- 2 large eggs
- 1 teaspoon vanilla extract
- 1/2 cup (120ml) buttermilk or milk
- 1/2 cup (120ml) boiling water
- 2-3 medium ripe pears, peeled, cored, and thinly sliced

For the Topping (optional):

- Powdered sugar, for dusting
- Whipped cream or vanilla ice cream, for serving

Instructions:

1. **Preheat the Oven:**
    1. Preheat your oven to 350°F (175°C). Grease and flour a 9-inch round or 10-inch square baking pan, or line it with parchment paper.
2. **Prepare the Cake Batter:**
    1. In a medium bowl, sift together the flour, cocoa powder, baking powder, baking soda, and salt. Set aside.
    2. In a large bowl, cream together the softened butter and granulated sugar until light and fluffy.
    3. Beat in the eggs one at a time, mixing well after each addition. Stir in the vanilla extract.
    4. Gradually add the dry ingredients to the butter mixture, alternating with the buttermilk, beginning and ending with the dry ingredients. Mix until just combined.
    5. Carefully fold in the boiling water until the batter is smooth. The batter will be thin, but this is normal.
3. **Prepare the Pears:**
    1. Arrange the thinly sliced pears evenly over the bottom of the prepared baking pan.
4. **Assemble the Cake:**
    1. Pour the chocolate batter over the pears in the pan, spreading it evenly.

       2. Gently tap the pan on the counter to remove any air bubbles.
5. **Bake the Cake:**
       1. Bake in the preheated oven for 35-45 minutes, or until a toothpick inserted into the center of the cake comes out clean and the top is set.
       2. If the cake starts to over-brown before it's fully baked, you can cover it loosely with aluminum foil.
6. **Cool and Serve:**
       1. Allow the cake to cool in the pan for 10 minutes before transferring it to a wire rack to cool completely.
       2. Dust with powdered sugar before serving, if desired.
       3. Serve the cake warm or at room temperature, optionally with whipped cream or vanilla ice cream.

Tips for Success:

- **Pears:** Use ripe but firm pears so they don't disintegrate during baking.
- **Buttermilk Substitute:** If you don't have buttermilk, you can use regular milk mixed with a tablespoon of lemon juice or vinegar.
- **Texture:** The batter is intentionally thin to ensure a moist cake. The pears will cook into the batter, creating a delightful texture.

This Pear Chocolate Cake combines the decadence of chocolate with the freshness of pears, resulting in a cake that's both rich and light. It's perfect for a special occasion or as a comforting dessert to enjoy with family and friends. Enjoy!

Apfel-Mandelkuchen (Apple Almond Cake)

Ingredients:

For the Cake:

- 1 1/2 cups (190g) all-purpose flour
- 1 teaspoon baking powder
- 1/2 teaspoon baking soda
- 1/4 teaspoon salt
- 1/2 cup (115g) unsalted butter, softened
- 1 cup (200g) granulated sugar
- 2 large eggs
- 1 teaspoon vanilla extract
- 1/2 cup (120ml) buttermilk or milk
- 1 1/2 cups (about 3 medium) peeled, cored, and chopped apples (such as Granny Smith or Honeycrisp)
- 1/2 cup (50g) sliced almonds

For the Almond Topping (optional):

- 1/4 cup (30g) sliced almonds
- 2 tablespoons granulated sugar
- 1 tablespoon unsalted butter, melted

For the Glaze (optional):

- 1/2 cup (60g) powdered sugar
- 2-3 tablespoons milk or lemon juice

Instructions:

1. **Preheat the Oven:**
    1. Preheat your oven to 350°F (175°C). Grease and flour a 9-inch round or 10-inch square baking pan, or line it with parchment paper.
2. **Prepare the Cake Batter:**
    1. In a medium bowl, sift together the flour, baking powder, baking soda, and salt. Set aside.
    2. In a large bowl, cream together the softened butter and granulated sugar until light and fluffy.
    3. Beat in the eggs one at a time, mixing well after each addition. Stir in the vanilla extract.
    4. Gradually add the dry ingredients to the butter mixture, alternating with the buttermilk, beginning and ending with the dry ingredients. Mix until just combined.
    5. Gently fold in the chopped apples until evenly distributed in the batter.
3. **Prepare the Almond Topping (if using):**

1. In a small bowl, combine the sliced almonds with granulated sugar and melted butter. Stir until the almonds are coated.
4. **Assemble the Cake:**
    1. Pour the batter into the prepared baking pan and smooth the top with a spatula.
    2. Sprinkle the almond topping evenly over the batter, if using.
5. **Bake the Cake:**
    1. Bake in the preheated oven for 35-45 minutes, or until a toothpick inserted into the center comes out clean and the top is golden brown.
    2. Allow the cake to cool in the pan for 10 minutes before transferring to a wire rack to cool completely.
6. **Prepare the Glaze (if using):**
    1. In a small bowl, whisk together the powdered sugar and milk (or lemon juice) until smooth. Adjust the consistency with more milk or powdered sugar if needed.
7. **Serve:**
    1. Once the cake has cooled, drizzle with the glaze if desired, or simply dust with powdered sugar.
    2. Slice and serve.

Tips for Success:

- **Apples:** Choose apples that are firm and not overly sweet, as they will provide a nice balance to the sweetness of the cake.
- **Texture:** For a chunkier texture, chop the apples into larger pieces. For a finer texture, you can grate the apples.
- **Almonds:** Toasting the almonds before adding them to the cake batter will enhance their flavor.

This Apple Almond Cake is a comforting and flavorful dessert that combines the sweetness of apples with the nutty crunch of almonds. It's a great way to use up apples and makes a wonderful treat for any occasion. Enjoy!

Käsekuchen mit Streuseln (Cheesecake with Crumbs)

Ingredients:

For the Crust:

- 1 1/2 cups (150g) graham cracker crumbs or digestive biscuit crumbs
- 1/4 cup (50g) granulated sugar
- 1/4 cup (60g) unsalted butter, melted

For the Streusel Topping:

- 1/2 cup (60g) all-purpose flour
- 1/2 cup (100g) granulated sugar
- 1/4 cup (50g) unsalted butter, cold and cubed
- 1/2 teaspoon ground cinnamon (optional)

For the Cheesecake Filling:

- 16 oz (450g) cream cheese, softened
- 1 cup (200g) granulated sugar
- 1 teaspoon vanilla extract
- 3 large eggs
- 1 cup (240ml) sour cream
- 1/4 cup (60ml) heavy cream
- 2 tablespoons all-purpose flour

Instructions:

1. **Preheat the Oven:**
    1. Preheat your oven to 350°F (175°C). Grease a 9-inch (23 cm) springform pan or line the bottom with parchment paper.
2. **Prepare the Crust:**
    1. In a medium bowl, combine the graham cracker crumbs, granulated sugar, and melted butter.
    2. Press the mixture firmly into the bottom of the prepared springform pan to form an even layer.
    3. Bake the crust in the preheated oven for 8-10 minutes, or until lightly golden. Remove from the oven and let it cool while you prepare the filling.
3. **Prepare the Streusel Topping:**
    1. In a medium bowl, mix together the flour, granulated sugar, and ground cinnamon (if using).
    2. Add the cold, cubed butter and use your fingers or a pastry cutter to work the butter into the dry ingredients until the mixture resembles coarse crumbs. Set aside.
4. **Prepare the Cheesecake Filling:**

1. In a large bowl, beat the softened cream cheese until smooth and creamy.
2. Add the granulated sugar and vanilla extract, and beat until combined.
3. Add the eggs one at a time, beating well after each addition.
4. Mix in the sour cream, heavy cream, and flour until smooth.
5. Pour the cheesecake filling over the cooled crust in the springform pan.

5. **Add the Streusel Topping:**
   1. Evenly sprinkle the streusel topping over the cheesecake filling.
6. **Bake the Cheesecake:**
   1. Bake in the preheated oven for 50-60 minutes, or until the center is set and the edges are slightly puffed. The center may still jiggle slightly, but it should not be liquid.
   2. Turn off the oven and let the cheesecake cool in the oven with the door slightly ajar for 1 hour. This helps prevent cracking.
7. **Cool and Chill:**
   1. Remove the cheesecake from the oven and refrigerate for at least 4 hours, or overnight, to fully set.
8. **Serve:**
   1. Once chilled and set, carefully remove the cheesecake from the springform pan.
   2. Slice and serve chilled.

Tips for Success:

- **Cream Cheese:** Make sure the cream cheese is fully softened before mixing to avoid lumps in the filling.
- **Baking:** If the top of the cheesecake starts to brown too much, you can cover it loosely with aluminum foil.
- **Crumbs:** For a more pronounced crust flavor, consider adding a bit of cinnamon to the crumb mixture.

This Cheesecake with Crumbs is a wonderful combination of creamy cheesecake and crunchy streusel, making it a standout dessert for any occasion. Enjoy this classic treat!

Hasselback-Kuchen (Hasselback Cake)

Ingredients:

For the Cake:

- 1 1/2 cups (190g) all-purpose flour
- 1 teaspoon baking powder
- 1/2 teaspoon baking soda
- 1/4 teaspoon salt
- 1/2 cup (115g) unsalted butter, softened
- 1 cup (200g) granulated sugar
- 2 large eggs
- 1 teaspoon vanilla extract
- 1/2 cup (120ml) buttermilk or milk

For the Topping:

- 3-4 medium apples or pears (such as Granny Smith or Bosc), peeled, cored, and thinly sliced
- 2 tablespoons granulated sugar
- 1 teaspoon ground cinnamon
- 2 tablespoons unsalted butter, melted

For the Glaze (optional):

- 1/4 cup (60ml) apricot or apple jam, warmed
- 1 tablespoon water

Instructions:

1. **Preheat the Oven:**
    1. Preheat your oven to 350°F (175°C). Grease and flour a 9-inch round or 10-inch square baking pan, or line it with parchment paper.
2. **Prepare the Cake Batter:**
    1. In a medium bowl, sift together the flour, baking powder, baking soda, and salt. Set aside.
    2. In a large bowl, cream together the softened butter and granulated sugar until light and fluffy.
    3. Beat in the eggs one at a time, mixing well after each addition. Stir in the vanilla extract.
    4. Gradually add the dry ingredients to the butter mixture, alternating with the buttermilk, beginning and ending with the dry ingredients. Mix until just combined.
3. **Prepare the Fruit Topping:**
    1. In a small bowl, toss the thinly sliced apples or pears with granulated sugar and ground cinnamon.

2. Arrange the fruit slices in a fan-like pattern on top of the cake batter. You can overlap them slightly, working from the outer edge toward the center.
4. **Bake the Cake:**
   1. Drizzle the melted butter over the arranged fruit slices.
   2. Bake in the preheated oven for 40-50 minutes, or until a toothpick inserted into the center of the cake comes out clean and the fruit is tender and caramelized.
   3. If the fruit starts to brown too quickly, you can cover the cake loosely with aluminum foil.
5. **Prepare the Glaze (optional):**
   1. In a small saucepan, heat the apricot or apple jam with water until it becomes liquid and smooth.
   2. Brush the warm glaze over the baked fruit topping to give it a shiny finish.
6. **Cool and Serve:**
   1. Allow the cake to cool in the pan for 10 minutes before transferring to a wire rack to cool completely.
   2. Slice and serve at room temperature or slightly warmed.

Tips for Success:

- **Fruit Slices:** Ensure that the fruit slices are as thin as possible for even cooking and a more delicate texture.
- **Cake Batter:** Do not overmix the batter to avoid a dense cake.
- **Glaze:** The glaze adds a beautiful shine and extra sweetness, but the cake is also delicious without it.

This Hasselback Cake is both a visual and culinary delight, perfect for impressing guests or enjoying as a special treat. The combination of moist cake and caramelized fruit makes for a delicious and elegant dessert. Enjoy!